Praise for *Tales from the Back Row* by Amy Odell

Wall Street Journal **"Year's Best Fashion Books"**
Named a Must-Read by *Bustle, Lenny Letter, POPSUGAR, Refinery29,*
theSkimm, US Weekly, **Lauren Conrad, and more!**

"Book Report 'A' rating . . . a witty and candid 'outsider's view from inside the fashion industry,' complete with an intimidating Anna Wintour encounter."

—*In Touch*

"Self-deprecating and funny."

—*The New York Times Book Review*

"In *Tales from the Back Row*, Odell delivers lively observations, wry commentary and several rip-roaringly funny anecdotes from her time in fashion, during which she climbed the ranks from party reporter to blogger at the Cut to her current position as editor of Cosmopolitan.com. . . . Odell is charmingly relatable and honest here. And the payoff is that readers get to go where they are unlikely ever to be on their own, into the belly of the Condé Nast building and Wintour's office."

—*The Washington Post*

"Odell's shamelessly dry, very smart wit is blogger-perfect, but it translates well into writing reverentially and intelligently about fashion. Whether or not you also love to hate or hate to love the fashion world, you will straight-up adore Amy Odell's candid observations and anecdotes culled from her years covering the runways."

—*Bustle*, "September 2015's Best Books"

"This delightful book of essays by Cosmopolitan.com editor Amy Odell pulls back the curtain and shows that it's not always so fabulous climbing the fashion ladder."

—*Refinery29*, "Fall's Most Highly Anticipated Nonfiction Reads"

"A funny, insightful debut."

—*Harper's Bazaar*

"A backstage pass to the intimidating, backbiting industry."

—*US Weekly*

"Amy Odell cuts through a lot of the bull in the fashion business and the fashion media in her witty new memoir, *Tales from the Back Row* . . . The book covers an amazing amount of ground without ever coming across as a fashion lecture. Odell keeps herself front and center as our guide and we learn what's what through her eyes and ears. . . . Odell is refreshingly down to earth and honest."

—*The Connecticut Post*

"Funny, insightful and relatable to pretty much anyone who works in media."

—*AM NY*

"A sharply amusing fashion memoir."

—*Kirkus Reviews*

"A great and almost natural comic narrative, laced with lots of name-dropping, will evoke chuckles—and a sigh of relief that there are no reader portraits."

—*Booklist*

"Just delicious."

—*Book Riot*

"In her first book, *Tales from the Back Row*, Amy Odell, editor of Cosmopolitan.com, gives an inside look at what a job in fashion journalism is like for us mere mortals. Odell talks about the fashion industry in a way the everyday fashion lover will understand—even those not interested in fashion will understand. She breaks the fashion industry down to the stitches, demystifying that entire world."

—Medium.com

"Whether you're interested in pursuing a career in publishing, public relations or design, or you're just fascinated with what *really* goes on behind-the-scenes without the usual sugarcoating, we'd say this is required reading."

—Fashionista.com

"If you haven't snagged any invites (to NYFW), let *Tales from the Back Row*, Cosmopolitan.com editor Amy Odell's first book, out now, transport you."

—*Trending NY*

"Hilarious, insightful, and smart. A must-read for anyone who wears clothes."

—Chelsea Handler

"*Tales from the Back Row* takes you from the hottest fashion shows to the coolest after parties, along the decidedly unglamorous roads Amy Odell travels to get there. Don't miss this terrific debut. It's better than landing the most coveted seat at fashion week."

—Lauren Weisberger, *New York Times* bestselling author of *Revenge Wears Prada* and *The Devil Wears Prada*

"Amy is one of my favorite people in the fashion industry. She's smart, stylish, and simply not a dick."

—Grace Helbig

"*Tales from the Back Row* is a delicious peek behind the curtain of fame and fashion. Amy Odell doesn't pull any punches—not at the industry, the celebrities circling it, or even at herself—and her insider dish will make you laugh out loud."

—The Fug Girls

TALES

from the

BACK ROW

AN OUTSIDER'S VIEW FROM INSIDE THE FASHION INDUSTRY

Amy Odell

SIMON & SCHUSTER PAPERBACKS
New York London Toronto Sydney New Delhi

Simon & Schuster Paperbacks
An Imprint of Simon & Schuster, Inc.
1230 Avenue of the Americas
New York, NY 10020

First Simon & Schuster trade paperback edition September 2016

SIMON & SCHUSTER PAPERBACKS and colophon are registered trademarks of Simon & Schuster, Inc.

For information about special discounts for bulk purchases, please contact Simon & Schuster Special Sales at 1-866-506-1949 or business@simonandschuster.com.

The Simon & Schuster Speakers Bureau can bring authors to your live event. For more information or to book an event contact the Simon & Schuster Speakers Bureau at 1-866-248-3049 or visit our website at www.simonspeakers.com.

Interior design by Joy O'Meara

Manufactured in the United States of America

1 3 5 7 9 10 8 6 4 2

The Library of Congress has cataloged the hardcover as follows:
Odell, Amy.
Tales from the back row : an outsider's view from inside the fashion industry / Amy Odell.—First Simon & Schuster hardcover edition.
pages cm
1. Odell, Amy. 2. Clothing trade—New York (State) —New York—Biography.
3. Clothing trade—Social aspects—New York (State)—New York. 4. Fashion—New York (State)—New York. 5. Fashion design—New York (State)—New York.
I. Title.
TT496.U62N763 2015
746.9'2097471—dc23   2015018051

ISBN 978-1-4767-4975-4
ISBN 978-1-4767-4976-1 (pbk)
ISBN 978-1-4767-4977-8 (ebook)

For my parents

Contents

CONTENTS

Introduction

Ugh, I *loved* it," said a man in navy trousers rolled up past his ankles to a spindly woman wearing heels that made her feet look like hulking bronze insects.

"I *lorved* it," she agreed in Italian-accented English. "My favoreet show so far. De ripped tights! De attitude! Ee deliver."

It was a cold and cloudy February Thursday in 2008, midday, and here I was in the bizarre and very intimidating position of exiting a fashion show in New York's meatpacking district—a post–*Sex and the City*–chic neighborhood characterized by nightclubs, $16 Bellinis, and Eurotrash. A young designer named Alexander Wang had titillated his audience with ripped black tights, leg warmers, and, evidently, some *very* exciting vests. This was Fashion Week, a biannual occurrence in New York City that lands like a tornado, sweeping up a whole bunch of fabulous weirdos, depositing them at one fashion show before picking them up and carrying them off to the next one. And so this repeats all day every day for eight days while everyone complains about it and non-fashion New Yorkers wonder why there are so many more traffic jams and really skinny people around.

I had been working in the fashion industry for, well, two days. I had just started my job as the first blogger at the Cut, *New York* magazine's website dedicated full-time to fashion coverage. I had no clue what distinguished a high-quality, fashionable pair of ripped tights from ripped tights without fashion world–altering significance. I thought I knew a lot about fashion, but as I exited that Alexander Wang show, I was beginning to realize that being obsessed with *Project Runway* makes one an expert in fashion as much as watching *The Bachelor* makes one an expert in prisoner psychology.

More than five years and countless fashion shows later, I was hired to edit the website for *Cosmopolitan,* which covers everything from politics to what to do with your leftover pizza (fold it in half and *put it in a waffle iron*, telling you). But fashion still fascinates me, and has had a greater effect on my life than any other beat I've been on, and not just because I can now look at a pair of ripped tights and tell whether or not they actually look cool or like they just came from an average person's Dumpster.

That day, I wanted to feel as moved by Alexander Wang's asymmetrical zippers as the real fashion people around me were. I could see by their pant-cuffing techniques and choices of footwear alone that they were capable of falling in love—a deep, moving love—with clothes, especially leather ones. These people looked at shoes and experienced the same emotions the average person does passing puppies in a window at a pet store: they fall all *over* themselves. Back then, I knew nothing about fashion, and therefore could not understand their reaction. *Project Runway*? Many feelings felt. Fashion? Just one: confusion.

Then, I felt about fashion shows and parties the way the editor of a prominent DJ magazine once told me he felt about teenage girls who go dance at raves for hours wearing little more than bras and panties. When I asked him why all the girls who go to dance-music concerts dress basically naked these days, he recalled one show where he found himself sitting with a direct view of a group of teenage girls, wearing bathing suits, underwear, or some variation thereof, stomachs, buttocks, and cleavage exposed in a pulsating cluster before him. *"Am I not supposed to look at this?"* he recalled thinking.

"Am I not supposed to look at this?" is something I, too, often wonder at fashion shows and parties. I can't help but look at human thighs as firm and slim and browned as breadsticks in an Olive Garden commercial, arrayed in front of me like an all-you-can-eat bottomless basket. Or gawk conspicuously at seemingly hideous denim and camel leather patchwork jumpsuits (I will find out I'm in the minority of fashion people who does not want one to wear tomorrow). Or feel jarred by the sight of celebrities showing up to 9:00 a.m. fashion shows in full cocktail wear, like they're not there to sit in a seat, but about to turn the letters around on *Wheel of Fortune.*

I see some things that others either choose to ignore or no longer notice. Like the thighs thinner than most arms. The desperation with which some people attire themselves in order to get photographed. The egos that seem to motivate so many people to do so many unnecessary things, like wear sunglasses indoors as though they are high on Ecstasy.

That is the stuff you're supposed to ignore, because within the industry, it's all just normal. *Outside* the industry, it's anything but.

· · ·

"Fashion," I soon learned, was different from "clothing."

At most fashion shows (and I'd only been to a few at this point) everyone acts as if the whole thing is about as exciting as vacuuming crumbs out of a couch. The fashion people can't wait to get out because they'll never be on time to their next show and everything about this is so exhausting and stressful. Lo, HOW HARD IT IS TO SPEND THE DAY GOING TO FASHION SHOWS. THE WOE. (*The woe.*)

And so, I felt that their reaction to the Alexander Wang show was different. This pair of ripped black tights was like smelling salts: it had stirred the bored, deadened insides of people who had looked at so many shoes in their careers that they were interested in only those that looked like a species deserving of its own Latin taxonomy. And I wanted to know why. What did these people know that allowed them to navigate—and dictate—the whims of an industry that has so much power over women in pursuit of a certain look? And why is what they themselves love so *strange*? And, ultimately, unattainable?

Starting out, I understood some things about the fashion business and its people (fashion people). I understood that fashion people liked to wear all-black because they consider it to be the most fashionable thing to wear, at all times, for any occasion. I also understood that they regarded waiting in line for anything as a plebeian activity they did not deserve to suffer through. I understood that they almost never ate hors d'oeuvres, even though they are, for some reason, always around. And I understood that when they're not totally bored by everything, they tend to convey emotions most strongly through single-word proclamations (see: "Obsessed!" "Dead!" "LOVE!").

But I also knew as soon as I hit the Fashion Week circuit in a pair of hole-free tights and my finest high school holdovers from Dillard's that I was not like them. Though I did believe lines were a thing to be avoided at all costs and saw no shame in pursuing the status necessary to gain the privilege of skipping them—airline miles to skip the plane line, being female and with *other* females to skip the nightclub line. But present me with a tray of thimble-sized "mac 'n' cheese cupcakes," and I am quite simply going to eat one.

Perhaps because of the differences between those who were born for this world and me, I found everything happening at fashion events perplexing and hugely intimidating and completely alien—the people, the clothes they wore, the clothes they refused to wear. They looked at certain shows as a religious experience. I looked at the same shows as a series of jumpsuits I would never wear.

I've since learned that this industry is defined by these people. When you see a celebrity wearing a designer dress on a magazine cover, you're not just looking at a specimen of fame encased in duchesse satin. You're seeing the work of the designer who created the dress, the stylist who told the celebrity to wear the dress, the hair and makeup people who made her look like she *belongs* in that dress, the editors who selected the celebrity and the dress as the emblem of taste in our time. On a less perceptible level, you are seeing the work of the various publicists who turned this celebrity into a star and who turned this designer into a label worthy of the star's body and magazine's most prime real estate. And you are seeing countless influencers of trends—not only the internet stars who cover the industry on a second-to-second basis, but also the trend forecasters who, two years ago, told everyone from the cosmetics companies who made the makeup to the designers themselves that everyone will wear moss green in eighteen months because of some high-level reasoning relating to the economy and a feeling in the air. They say a picture is worth a thousand words—they're wrong: in fashion, it's actually worth a thousand people. And the thing that binds them isn't just the emblem of taste in our time, but also the eccentricity and distance from reality that movies like *Zoolander* caricature so well.

Some of these fashion people go from ugly ducklings to beautiful and eccentric fashion-famous swans; others emerged from the womb as full-grown adults in stilettos and leather pants who refuse to consume dairy products. Not me, though. Rest assured, I came out of the womb with ZERO style and a strong affinity for dairy products.

That's not to say I wasn't interested in clothes. Being a female with every cartoon Disney movie on VHS, I was positively obsessed with sparkly things and princess fashion. When I was around six, the children's shoe store where I bought all my Keds carried a pair of very glittery flats that I just *had* to have. When I first laid eyes upon them, I looked at my mom and exclaimed, "Those are my shoes!" No shoes had ever been destined to be worn by both Liberace and a six-year-old girl quite like these.

I couldn't stop thinking about them. But my parents wouldn't buy them for me right away. They were testing me—they said I didn't "need" them, but I figured they just wanted me to prove my commitment to this footwear, so I begged. I fantasized about how *good* life would be once I had these shoes. My feet would be so SPARKLY—how could my mother and father fail to see the immediate and lasting payoff of me owning glitter shoes I would ruin on the playground and grow out of in a few months? Some people don't understand anything.

One day, when they had realized I would not relent, they came around and agreed to buy me the glitter shoes.

We went back to the shoe store but they didn't have the multi-colored glitter style I had been obsessing over in my size. The sales-person offered to order them for us and brought out a red style for me to try for fit.

No social injustice was greater in my kindergartener world than learning I'd have to WAIT for my glitter shoes. I had already waited long enough and flat-out refused to wait anymore. Couldn't the shoe store lady see this? Couldn't my dad?

I put on the red glitter shoes and skipped around the store. I didn't want to take them off and I *especially* didn't want to wait for my multicolored ones to arrive.

"I'll take these," I informed the saleswoman.

"Now, Amy, don't you want the multicolored ones?" my dad said. "We'll order the other ones and you'll have them next week. You won't like these as much."

He turned to the counter, and I tried to convince myself that I really wanted the red ones and these old people were wrong. I clicked my heels when no one was looking because I'd seen *The Wizard of Oz* and knew that if I tapped my sparkly shoes together I'd be transported to a magical land where everyone understood the power of sparkly shoes and a giant cat would talk to me. That's the power of fashion. No one really understands the magical forces behind it, only that it has the power to take you to faraway, other-worldly places. Or, as the people at Fashion Week so often remind me, sometimes it just makes you look like you came from one.

In middle school, I really began to see how clothing could dis-tinguish certain groups of people. Now let me be very clear: *I was not cool.* The hot football players were not sending me secret ad-mirer roses on Valentine's Day. I was not in my high school's club of "Senior Girls," composed mostly of cheerleaders or dance team members, who would shoe polish football players' cars with hearts and clouds and decorate their rooms before games. (I know—*feminism*; don't get me started.) However, I was very much aware that the people who did also had perfect Abercrombie cutoffs and wore their hair in messy ponytails just to show how little they tried to look good. (The first law of looking good is you generally have to try to look good; the second law of looking good is making sure you don't *look* like you tried.) I first saw in grade school that social status and clothing were inextricably linked. Studying and analyzing this truth *professionally* would become my job as a fashion journalist. Because fashion is not just about dresses, it's about so much more—it's about who can afford the dresses, who is famous or important enough to borrow the dresses, where the dresses can even be worn because they're so outlandish and fancy that they'd look a fool in every single place nonfamous, non-fashion people spend time.

After high school, I moved to New York to attend New York University, where, in between going to nightclubs to make up for how dorky and book-bound I was in high school, I studied journalism. As an intern at the *New York Observer*, I was desperate for clips and ended up covering red carpet events to get them. I went to fashion show after fashion show and fashion party after fashion party, trying to interview the grown glitter-shoe-wearing adults on the inside and make sense of it all from the outside.

I learned that the fashion industry accords status by row. The more important you are, the better your seat at fashion shows. Anna Wintour, editor in chief of *Vogue*, gets the best seat—front row, center, always—because she's the most important person in the industry. As *Vogue* documentarian R. J. Cutler said, "Well, you can make a film in Hollywood without Steven Spielberg's blessing, and you can publish software in Silicon Valley without Bill Gates's blessing, but it's pretty clear to me that you can't succeed in the fashion industry without Anna Wintour's blessing." Anna gets to do whatever she wants at Fashion Week, even more so than the other forty-nine people who get to do whatever they want. She gets to go inside and sit in her seat before the venue is open. She gets to go backstage and see the clothes at her leisure and take precedence over everyone else who needs to go backstage and schmooze with the designer. Other people who get to sit on the front row include more *Vogue* editors, sometimes as many as five or six. And sometimes there are so many people from *Vogue* a few have to sit on the *second* row behind Anna, which is always slightly scandalous to the people who have to turn what happens at Fashion Week into stories and blog posts. "*Vogue* Editor So and So Relegated to SECOND ROW SEAT," headlines blare. I don't understand why six people from one magazine need to be at one fashion show. I don't know if they're just there to be supportive of the designer in a self-acknowledgment of their own importance ("*Everyone* from *Vogue* was there," someone might say afterward) or if they're working (but how much work can six people *do* at one fashion show?). And is that much work on one fashion show actually needed? I really don't know the answers. The one thing I do know is that it is remarkable how calm and thin all the *Vogue* people look all the time. Fashion Week stresses most people out, but being very well dressed and slim hides that stress remarkably well.

Aside from team *Vogue*, front-row people include editors from other magazines (though I never notice as many as *Vogue*'s lineup), top buyers from important stores like Bergdorf Goodman and Barneys and Saks, critics from places like the *New York Times* and the *Wall Street Journal*, and celebrities. You know a celebrity is entering the venue not because you can see them from your z-row seat, oh no, but because celebrities, especially really, really famous ones, enter last, surrounded by approximately 112 people who form at once a devotional and protective circle around said celebrity, with a uniform density that is maintained as the celebrity traverses the couple dozen yards between her car and her seat. It's as though the celebrity has just had spinal surgery and is walking for the first time down the hospital corridor with the help of a well-dressed, especially hulking physical therapist on each arm. I have seen Beyoncé move around fashion shows in this very way, which has the effect of making her high heels look really, truly, just that dangerous.

People in the front row dress spectacularly in clothes that cost more than most mortgages. They text regularly with celebrities, whether or not they are one. Front-row people have photographers orbiting them like their own moons.

No one orbits me (see: aforementioned unfashionable wardrobe), but I *was* almost run over in the middle of Fifth Avenue this one time because someone wanted to take a picture of me holding a borrowed Chanel bag. The rest of the time I slip amid the crowd unseen. But that's just what life is like when your seat is somewhere near Canada, in the back row. You're allowed in; you're just not on the inside.

This book is about the people who power this industry—the bloggers, trendsetters, designers, celebrities, editors, and models. It's about what it's like to begin a career in the world populated by these very people, with whom I thought I had little in common but an innate attraction to sparkly shoes.

This is an unpretentious look (real talk) at a world that befuddles onlookers, a world of exclusivity, shameless self-promotion, and extreme ideals of what is and isn't beautiful. The tales that follow are neither mockery nor outright tell-all—I enjoy fashion too much to write it off as one never-ending *Zoolander* movie, though I wouldn't say that film's depiction of male models and fashion generally is *entirely* inaccurate. But I also never happened to witness anyone snorting cocaine off hand mirrors backstage.

This industry runs itself in such a way as to make consumers, particularly women, feel bad about themselves—for being too poor, too fat, too unattractive, too tasteless, too conventional. I am not immune to this. It's part of what drew me to this business in the first place. The fashion industry, in many ways, is a study in how deeply we long to stand out in order to fit in. A shrink once told me that we spend our energy trying to "fit in" with those around us up until around college, when we try to make ourselves stand out. Really, this is just another version of fitting in, because everyone's doing it. The fashion industry bears just about zero resemblance to college, except perhaps for this and how easy it is to get drunk every night if that's what you feel like doing. At Fashion Week, that desire is so pronounced that it's no big deal to see grown women with glittery pineapples protruding from their heads. (These head ornaments are called fascinators, and they are most commonly seen on British royals and socialites at horse races, but some fashion people can really pull them off.)

. . .

I'm not part of the in-crowd. If I were, I don't think I'd be able to write about it any differently than the pages of *Vogue* (not real talk), which serves primarily as a purveyor of the illusion of fashion, rather than a decoder of it. What magazines like *Vogue* forget or simply can't tell you is that *there is nothing normal about this business.* Crocodile backpacks that cost $50,000 and come with a designer label aren't just something you mix into your Hamptons wardrobe, and not just because you don't have a Hamptons wardrobe but because they're bizarre, and the people who become attached to these things are sometimes equally unusual. Somewhere along the way, expressing just that became a big no-no for those who wanted to remain on the inside.

And so the fashion world consists of these people, like those two at that Alexander Wang show, who loved that pair of ripped tights and that leather vest, who exalt the disco pineapple fascinator, and who never seem to question the source of their feelings for these items of clothing or challenge the context in which these feelings arise. That can be a scary job, and I'm not afraid to do it.

I did end up purchasing a vest from that Wang collection at a sale some months afterward. But if I showed up anywhere wearing it with a pair of ripped tights and asked someone what they think of me, I'm pretty sure they'd just say, "Less."

· 1 ·

Bloggers

MASTERING THE LAME FLAMINGO

Landing a job as a full-time fashion writer was a glamorous dream I never expected to fulfill. Especially after I got fired from my first job. I was an editorial assistant at Jewcy, a website about Jewish stuff that was supposed to reach cool young people but ended up not reaching a large audience at all and shut down before being relaunched by people who could find an actual audience for the thing. My job involved sitting in a cramped office, filing invoices, and assisting someone who was sort of weird and not particularly warm. This was New Media 101, and I got the $400-a-week paycheck, benefits not included, to show for it. I'm pretty sure that even though this was the kind of real, high-value work college is supposed to groom you for, I made less than I did at my high school hostess job at a Tex-Mex chain. *Vogue* editor-in-chief Anna Wintour, who was fired from *Harper's Bazaar*, once said everyone should get fired once because "it's a great learning experience." I agree: you should get fired once because it *is* a great learning experience. For instance, if you didn't grow up buying full-price Pucci like a social-ite, you might have to learn how to live on the same amount of money your employed friends spend on lattes.

It also, theoretically, teaches you how not to get fired again.

There's a good chance that getting fired will be the best thing that ever happened to you. No matter how excited I've been to quit a job and move on to the next, I've always been terrified to quit. When I hostessed at that local Tex-Mex joint, the restaurant manager knew I would quit when I left for college, yet still I was nervous to tell him I was leaving. Having the unpleasant "I quit" conversation feels like telling someone, "No one likes you." So a boss asking you to leave a job—and it's probably one you hate; most people who get fired don't love the thing they're getting fired from (How could you? They're firing you!)—only saves you the extreme awkwardness of actually quitting. It also forces you to find something better as quickly as possible, instead of pussyfooting around about your job search because you've settled into a routine of G-chatting for six hours a day and doing work for just two, while making enough money to afford Bravo, possibly also HBO.

I was pretty lucky because after I got fired from Jewcy, I assisted, reported, and wrote five-sentence-long magazine articles as a freelancer for several months, and then *New York* magazine hired me to start its fashion blog, the Cut. This was the terrifying beginning of my career as a fashion journalist.

I should say this job didn't just fall from the sky and into my lap. That's just not how opportunities work, unless you are Paris Hilton in 2005 (which is not an advisable situation anyway, since you'd have to go everywhere wearing a neon loincloth and clear stilettos). I had been running around Manhattan asking celebrities awkward questions at cocktail parties as a freelance party reporter for

New York magazine. Picture a girl in T. J. Maxx trying to interrupt Elle Macpherson's conversation in the middle of the private lounge of a $500-a-night hotel. (Macpherson must have sensed my deep longing to interview her about summer flings, the subject of the film we were feting, because as soon as she finished with her conversation, she turned and fled.) I had been doing this for nearly a year, so *New York* magazine had a sense of my skills. Also, I had a competing offer to run another fashion blog, which I told them about in hopes they'd offer me a full-time job. Voilà. As soon as someone *else* wanted me, they decided to consider me for their top-secret fashion blogger position. Pro tip: the best way to make someone want you is to make someone else want you more.

Just hours after I told my party-reporting editor about the competing offer, the editor of NYmag.com called me and said something like, "We want to start a fashion blog. Do you want to try out to be our fashion blogger?" He may as well have asked me if, moving forward, I'd like to get around town exclusively by unicorn. *Oh! Oh! Yes, I do! I do I do!!!* I could not believe that I had been offered a full-time job at NYmag.com, a highly respected publication. I was so afraid of becoming a failure that to have any work, much less an absolute dream writing job at the only magazine I was dying to work for, felt unreal. Even if I would be blogging about fashion.

"I would be interested in that, yes," I said into the phone using my spa voice. I happened to be rushing through SoHo to crash a friend's midmorning kickboxing class with an expired guest pass. I felt like one of those highly enviable ladies who run around wearing yoga outfits in the middle of the day because instead of office work, they take barre class and buy kale at Whole Foods. But now, with an audition to become *New York* magazine's first fashion blogger, I turned right around and climbed back up the six flights of stairs to my apartment to hunker down with my cat and *The View* (poor man's barre class) to start working.

. . . . .

At this point in my career, I felt fairly confident in my fashion knowledge because I had interviewed Tim Gunn a few times and had seen every episode of *Project Runway*. This—along with searching "fashion" in Google News—surely gave me the credentials I needed to complete the writing samples I had to turn in as my tryout for the role. I would later learn I knew absolutely nothing about fashion. Or blogging. But somehow, I faked my way through the interview process well enough to get a job offer. I tried to be all calm and cool about it when I got the call.

"Oh, thanks so much," I said, reverting to spa voice. "Can I think it over and call you back?"

Then I called my parents to shout, "OH MY GOD I GOT IT! THE JOB EVERY GIRL WOULD KILL FOR! [INSERT MORE *THE DEVIL WEARS PRADA* REFERENCES]!!!!" This was a dream. The royal wedding of jobs. All those awkward celebrity encounters had finally gotten me somewhere! And also: fuck that dickhead who fired me!

Something like three minutes later, I just couldn't take it any longer and lunged toward the phone. I had this odd feeling that if I didn't say yes it might go away. "I accept!!!" I told my future editor, now on the edge of hysteria. I've since learned that job offers aren't like people you've slept with or cupcakes—they do not just disappear. I couldn't wait to tell the people I was working with at *Condé Nast Traveler*, where I had recently accepted a freelance three-day-a-week job assisting the sole web editor, that I had to quit to go become NYmag.com's first fashion blogger. The vocally fashion-obsessed editorial assistant who sat behind me and acted like I didn't exist would be shocked. The glee this filled me with was almost enough to counteract the nervousness I had about my writing abilities: how was I ever going to be as good or funny every single day as the existing and enormously talented NYmag.com blogging team?

I started my coveted fashion blogging job at NYmag.com in February 2008, right before Fall Fashion Week. "What an exciting time to start!" everyone said. Well, no—what a terrifying time to start. I had *two* days to learn everything about fashion, and blogging. I can't even memorize a Britney Spears song in two days.

People who wrote for the internet, referred to broadly at the time as "bloggers," were just beginning to earn legitimacy in the fashion world. On January 31, 2008, the *New York Times* published a story about the rise of beauty bloggers, boldly stating, "the cosmetics industry has stopped seeing bloggers as bottom feeders." (Of course, this feels hilarious now that beauty vloggers are millionaires . . .)

The same was true for some fashion bloggers. The term can apply to all kinds of different people, many of whose worth was debated intensely. Fashion bloggers are like the global warming of the fashion industry—their impact only selectively acknowledged despite their undeniable existence. At this time, a debate was raging in the fashion industry about a blogger's place in the industry. Did they deserve the front-row seats they had started getting? Most famously, Bryanboy sat front row at a Dolce & Gabbana show with a laptop, which really sent people into a frenzy. But not long after that, when then thirteen-year-old fashion blogger Tavi Gevinson sat front row at the Dior Couture show (wearing a gigantic, view-obstructing bow on her head, no less), the raised eyebrows turned to outright vitriol. Industry lifers couldn't understand how a teenager could burst onto the scene with a website, a dream, and a cute outfit and be awarded status they believed it should take decades to earn. Yet, you can see how easy it is to get confused about bloggers, firstly because it's confusing that taking photos of oneself wearing clothes now translates to, for a very lucky few, a lucrative career path. But this is only one kind of fashion blogger, for a few varieties exist:

1. *Journalists who happen to write for blogs.* This is my category. I'm a journalist whose medium happens to be the internet—a "blog," or "vertical" (fancy name for "section of a website that probably has its own tab at the top").

2. *Personal-style bloggers.* The people who post to the internet photos of themselves wearing clothes. The most fully formed personal-style blogs also treat viewers to a broader look at their subjects' lives. Think: photos of the inside of a hotel room, closet porn, this vintage store I went to this one time, cupcakes I thought were really pretty. These bloggers are bang-up stylists, own the best clothes, and eat the best baked goods, and I am jealous of all of them.

3. *Fashion fans who chronicle their fandom online.* Due to the independent nature of their sites, bloggers can create their own journalistic standards. Whereas many news outlets have rules about not accepting expensive gifts or free trips, independent bloggers can accept as many free gifts and trips as they want (if a blogger reviews a product they receive for free, FTC regulations require that the blogger disclose the product was a gift). The more gifts they

get, the better off they are, because who running an indie website really has the money to fly to São Paolo Fashion Week? And if you're in the business of sharing photos of yourself wearing clothes and aren't independently wealthy, where would you be without free or heavily discounted clothes with which to continually update your look? For this type of blogger, the consequence of receiving so much free stuff is that you pretty much have to cover all of it favorably or only feature stuff you truly love. So you end up with a fan site. I don't see this as much different from fashion magazines like *Vogue* or *Harper's Bazaar* that primarily promote the goods of their advertisers and cover things they love in the most— if at times, painfully—positive fashion. These sites are often very personality driven, even if they're not solely about how a certain person dresses.

4. *Instagram "celebs."* People with half a million followers, who are known better for that than anything else. They might have a blog, too, but their agents (because fashion blogging has become so weirdly lucrative and fame making, it now requires agents) tout their impressively robust Instagram followings as chief among their talents.

5. *Street-style photographers.* The most famous street-style photographers, like Phil Oh, Scott "the Sartorialist" Schuman, and Tommy Ton, got their start by posting to their own sites photos they took of people wearing outfits. Though photographers of their caliber now get a lot of high-paying commercial work, they're still called bloggers because they still update their websites—the main reason they came to be known in the first place. But they're really not bloggers in my mind so much as photojournalists. And they've become remarkably powerful—they sit front row at shows and get paid tens of thousands of dollars and up to shoot major ad cam-

paigns. What's more, getting photographed by one of them has become a true accomplishment. Wearing an oversized angora coat and man loafers to a fashion show, catching the eye of the Sartorialist, getting photographed by him, and then seeing your photo land on his site is the street-style version of admission to Harvard. An irrefutable nod to your utmost talent in dressing yourself.

The distinction between bloggers (the lesser) and other print media people (more legitimate, allegedly) is not only disappearing but actually reversing. Whereas they used to begrudgingly award bloggers and vloggers standing tickets and didn't care about that thing called Instagram, now brands practically beg internet stars to show up to events and fashion shows and Instagram something— anything! If a PR person overhears you saying "That tiny coffee cup is cute; we should Instagram that!" they will come running up to you and ask if a waiter can bring one over on a private tray with its own thumbnail-sized coordinating donut. Practically every professional writer and photographer in the world now works on something that could qualify as a blog and, therefore, could be categorized as a blogger. It's impossible to work in media in any form now and not put your work on the internet in some way. Yet at the same time, putting myself and the Blonde Salad (yes, that's a real personal-style blogger) and Phil Oh in the same category is like seeing dolphins and whales and mermaids jumping around in the ocean and calling them all "fish."

We need to implement new distinctions for "new media" people. As much I would like it to be my job, I am never going to succeed in making a career out of posting photos of myself wearing different outfits for people to enthuse over on the internet.

As for my personal style, it progressed slower than the speed of fossilization. When I started at the Cut, I knew as much about fashion as I did about gardening. Just as I knew soil is required to grow vegetables, some of which grow *above*ground and some of which grow *below*ground, I knew that people wear clothes. I knew that really expensive ones with price tags affixed to labels by leather strings were more likely to be considered "fashion" than Jeggings with clear MMMMMMMM stickers running down the legs. For months when I started, I would get up before seven each morning so that I could read every word in *Women's Wear Daily* to figure out what mattered the most in the fashion world that day. I could read enough to learn about the fashion business and how it worked and all that. I could figure out which designers worked at which labels, which labels people cared about the most, and what the trends were in everything from online retail strategy to spring denim. But I could not nearly as easily adopt a sense of personal style that said, "I am a person who understands fashion and excels at getting dressed. Do worship my choice of blouse." I was very cavelady about it: "This is shirt, this is pants, this is outfit." I used to wear this one white knit top with a tattoo print-esque design on it (shhh!) that had three-quarter-length bell sleeves. I had not yet switched to skinny jeans, so I wore said top with boot-cut Abercrombie jeans I'd owned since high school—the "worn in" kind that looked like they had been used as a rag to wash hippos before they became pants. (This was the hot look for seventeen-year-olds in Austin, Texas.) I wore Reef flip-flops made of fuzzy leopard-printed material. In terms of an everyday outfit for a person who would leave her house, it was perfectly fine in that it *clothed* me. But as an outfit for a person who would have to go to fashion shows and write about them, it was *embarrassing*. Like arriving at a wedding and not realizing your nipples are showing until you get there, and then you spend the next three hours wondering if anyone else can tell. Visible nipples would have been preferable to my tattoo prints and bell sleeves. At least then I'd have something in common with runway models, who I'm sure would prefer to wear sheer clothing than be seen in my old clothes on a runway.

But I'm not a stylist—I'm a writer and editor. It's not necessarily my job to know how to put really interesting outfits together. It's my job to understand trends, interview designers and models and celebrities, and to piece it all together for various blog items for my readers. I had to look professional, yes, and ideally sort of stylish, but I didn't necessarily need to know that the black-and-white leopard Cavalli top goes perfectly with those Lucite-heeled neon-trimmed Marni shoes and that pair of high-waisted jean shorts with the Chanel brooch on the upper right ass cheek.

I loved getting to riff and joke all day about celebrity clothing lines and J. Lo's sequined body stockings. I loved taking interviews and turning them into stories. I love writing about almost anything, really. But I am not a personal-style blogger, and I do not possess the same talents as Rumi "Fashiontoast" Neely, who is one of the original stars. She shot a series a few years back I'll always remember. She was wearing white and sashaying down a dark road holding a dream catcher. This is her work. Put on a ridiculously cool outfit, pose somewhere telegenic with a dream catcher or meal of fast food or one of her fluffy cats, repeat. She's managed to make a handsome career out of living her life as though it was one giant fashion editorial aka making her followers (me) wildly jealous of her life and taste. She ended up starring in a campaign for Forever 21. She has an agent. She's a jet-setter.

What I find people are usually referring to when they say "fashion bloggers," are people like Fashiontoast, or the Man Repeller (who models clothing that women love but that—wait for it— repels men), and Sea of Shoes (who, well, actually does the same thing). They are personal-style bloggers who operate independent sites, formatted like blogs. Some brands are really into having these bloggers come to Fashion Week and will organize them all in the front row the way I imagine Martha Stewart's flavored salt collection to be arranged attractively in the foreground of her spice cupboard. Brands seem to think that putting a bunch of bloggers in the front row will make a statement about how digitally savvy they are. But this says very little: seating a bunch of personal-style bloggers together in one place just means that that brand was able to print out the names of the most successful independently employed professional clothes wearers and tape them to some adjoining chair backs.

These bloggers are valuable in terms of publicizing certain brands. They have loyal followings that buy the items they link to or wear. And they're often "safe" because they generally cover everything positively. I was not a visible "face" in the industry and am not guaranteed to be positive about everything, so I get a great view of these bloggers from my seat twelve rows behind them, in the back row. I look upon these beautiful, ornately dressed people in envy, marveling at how I'd never think to wear two sheer blouses at once.

What's interesting about the bloggers' rush to the front row is how quickly they're displacing print media. Some of these bloggers have more significant—and probably more valuable—web presences than some legacy media brands. And you wonder why that is when these magazines have at least a couple dozen people on staff, and these blogs are run by maybe one person plus, arguably, whoever takes their pictures. Why some magazine websites aren't met with the same enthusiasm as ManRepeller.com is an embarrassment to these brands, which have, presumably, many, many more resources than a girl with a computer, a dream, and an affinity for fabulous shoes.

It's not like people like Sea of Shoes have taken Anna Wintour's front-row seat (LOL, no), but they might end up sitting across from her, which suggests they're of fairly similar importance as far as fashion world personalities go. Anna is surely more powerful, but she and the Seas of Shoeses of this world do have one significant thing in common: they're recognizable. They have a look. They're street-style photographer bait, whether they like it (Sea of Shoes) or not (Anna, seemingly). Street-style publicity is important because it helps make someone a personality, and the more of a personality you are, the more valuable you become. The bloggers seem to like street-style attention, for the most part, but they don't have much choice because it's essential to their brands. Meanwhile, for people like Anna, who walks past photographers as though it's just started raining and she can't wait to get inside, getting to wherever one's going is always more important than getting photographed going there. Anna is part of the group who shows up for the work itself, but for the new guard of fashion internet celebs, getting attention for showing up is part of the work.

Street style has become VERY intense at Fashion Week. It can feel like the paparazzi stalking Britney Spears in the weeks leading up to her head-shaving meltdown, except Fashion Week people don't scream at the street-style photographers for taking their pictures. Rather, they *invite* it by dressing elaborately and out of season and making themselves as available as a hot dog vendor outside show venues. I once came across a serious street-style photograph, by esteemed street-style photographer Mr. Newton, of a woman who happened to be a fashion blogger, "having lunch at the Seagram Building" in Manhattan on a Monday, wearing a sheer black blouse with nothing underneath. You could see all of her boobs, so it was like she was topless, and one imagined if she was indeed just on a lunchtime stroll, there would be lots of bankers in suits gathering around, staring at her boobs. I remember wondering, *Is this what street style has come to? The painfully stylish look is so done that people have to be NUDE to get photographed?*

It used to be that people who had clearly styled their outfits *just so* would linger around fashion events pretending to be engaged in meaningful conversations with friends they see so infrequently that 90 percent of their interactions are air-kissing. And then if they were dressed right, a street-style photographer would notice their *fab* outfit, and they'd be like, "Oh, me? You want to photograph me? OKAY, I GUESS I HAVE TIME! *Enchanté, Josephine,* but IT'S TIME FOR MY MOMENT!" And then they'd pose with one leg bent inward a little bit like they'd practiced it. Now, swarms of street-style paparazzi and being photographed for that little corner of the internet has become such a *fact* at Fashion Week that it's now perfectly acceptable to show up dressed really bizarrely and flashily and just stand there until people gather around you to photograph you. You couldn't find a more perfect relic of this narcissistic internet age.

. . .

People who go to Fashion Week sometimes dress just to get photographed. This does not mean people were necessarily dressing more thoughtfully or more creatively or (dare I even suggest the concept) more *practically*, but now they seem to dress just purely outlandishly, wearing clothing just for the sake of ornamentation and spectacle. As I started my second year at the Cut, I noticed that's how it worked: the stranger and flashier you looked—the more garish of a trend cocktail you could turn your body into—the more likely you were to get shot by these photographers. Runway clothes often work the same way: you see so many "normal" outfits as a person who works in the fashion business, that only the weird stuff becomes interesting and the so-weird-it's-borderline-not-clothing stuff becomes the only apparel that can possibly unhinge the extreme boredom brought on by most fashion shows that suckles the life straight from the teat of a fashion person's soul. Standing out—and I mean *really* standing out—becomes the new normal. The *good* thing about the street-style nonsense is that you get even more spectacular people watching than you'd get without it. Women end up going to fashion shows wearing stiletto sandals and chiffon skirts with no tights in February, or with glittery pineapples affixed to their heads, or with hair dyed to look gray instead of the other way around, or with big furry neon tails attached to their purses or slung around their necks because they're Louis Vuitton and Prada and therefore elevated from completely absurd items of excess to *so on-trend*. If a well-styled Fashion Week person got off the plane in 99 percent of the places on the rest of the earth, they'd be treated like aliens, of this I'm certain. Because that's how you fit in in this industry: wear something that would look insane just about everywhere that is not Fashion Week.

I once undertook an experiment to see if I could get photographed. At this point, I had three years at the Cut on my résumé: I understood the secret salt of the personal-style blogger. So I decided to go to the shows one day wearing a street-style costume. Ideally, I'd end up with a story about how street-style stardom boils down to a few things that don't necessarily bespeak one's *totes fab* style, but rather a sanitized version of looking ridiculous. My friend at work, Diana, a market editor, tried to call in a bunch of spectacular designer things for me to wear. This being Fashion Week, no one was interested in lending me an outfit because I'm not Madonna (breaking news) and they had actual important shows to put on—and here the back-row girl wants to borrow something? Though just about everyone we asked had negative interest in getting back to us to even reject us, we did manage to get Miu Miu to loan us a pair of open-toed glitter booties. But as the days dragged on and the window of time in which I had to pull off this experiment closed, I became increasingly anxious.

Day three of Fashion Week arrived. This is one of the most important days of New York Fashion Week, because designers Prabal Gurung, Alexander Wang, and Joseph Altuzarra all usually show. Often this is a busy day of actual work for me (reporting and writing about what happens that day, by which I mean *willing things to happen* because usually nothing worth writing about happens when all that's at stake is a bunch of people sitting in a room watching skinny tall girls walk back and forth wearing stuff), which leaves little time for self-indulgent outfit planning.

On day three, Prabal Gurung often has the first big show of the day. He is a really fabulous human being who remembers people and is always extra-kind when he speaks to them, but not in a fake, meeting-your-friend's-other-bridesmaids sort of way that makes you want to fork yourself. Before the show that year, I was on the list for a backstage interview, as was then *New York Times* critic Cathy Horyn, so I had to wait.

Like moviemaking, *waiting* is a big part of Fashion Week. If you're not waiting backstage for a designer or headsetted person to find you important enough to speak to, you're waiting to get inside a show venue, or waiting in your seat for a show to start. Most shows start, on average, half an hour late. Which doesn't make sense because, you may wonder, how long could it take to comb a girl's hair, fill in her eyebrows, and slip her into a dress? Forever, actually. It takes until the end of time to do these things. Partly because the models just came from a show where they had their hair painted with liquid clay and their entire eye sockets coated with red glitter. So that has to be undone before their hair, makeup, and nails can be done all over again for the show you're waiting to see. Then the designer has to finish visiting with important fashion critics like Cathy Horyn, before he finishes dressing his models and regarding them and so forth. Also, he has to wait for his seats to fill up, because often attendees are late because they had to preen for some cameras and have no expectation of these things starting on time anyway. (Some designers can afford to start on time, because everything revolves around them, and the guests are the ones who will really feel stupid if they are late and miss the show, but this is only, like, two people.)

Luckily, while I waited, I bumped into Bryanboy, one of the original fashion bloggers who dresses quite fabulously and gets photographed at fashion nonsense all the time. I filled him in on my scheme and asked him what he thought I should wear to actually pull this off. Bryanboy had borrowed a few beautiful designer things, including the colorful top he was wearing, to wear to the shows. I remember him telling me he thought street-style dressing had become so *extreme* that only the absolute most cutting-edge of all clothing would make an impact on photographers in a given season, unless they already knew you as a street-style celebrity. What is the most cutting-edge apparel in all the land? Well, possibly couture—the world's most expensive, entirely handmade clothes, that only qualify as couture when they are actually certified by a French council. But there exists a league of clothes arguably even more cutting-edge than couture, and that is next season's clothes. Meaning, the clothes we were seeing on the runways right *now* that wouldn't hit stores for average women to buy for another several months. I was beginning to despair. Dresses don't just go straight from a runway to my body because, again, I'm not Madonna. How would I turn myself into a street-style parody without doing something embarrassing like showing up wearing a coconut bra and leggings? It was the only way I might ever look street-style strange enough.

Just as Gurung finished his chat with Cathy, celebrity stylist and designer Rachel Zoe came bounding into the venue. Well, Rachel Zoe didn't have her name put on a list to go backstage, but I remember that she did seem to have free rein to run around wherever she wanted that season, devoid of the seven layers of badges, wristbands, and Hogwarts-level clearance the plebeians like me need to get backstage to do their work.

She wore a black suit with flared pants and a multistrand gold bracelet and her signature oversized dark sunglasses, with a QVC tag hanging around her neck (she was showing her QVC line that season and had to wear credentials for *that*, but not this). And, whereas badges were outfit death for most not-famous people, she was probably getting her face photographed off anyway. But that's what you get when you're a burgeoning icon with an iconic look and a Bravo show.

Gurung slipped away from Cathy to greet Zoe, who was in a big rush to get back to QVC. Zoe deserved his enthusiasm because she helped make him a big deal by dressing her clients (Demi Moore, Kate Hudson) in Gurung's pieces when he was relatively unknown. Their love, as it manifested that day, is that of two people in a long-distance relationship who just want to do it as soon as they see each other. Zoe greeted Gurung with a slew of exclamations involving giggling and *OH MY GOD*s and lots of squealing. He did the same, they uttered each other's names orgasmically. Mid-embrace, Gurung lifted Zoe's lithe body off the ground, she wrapped her legs around his waist, and there was more giggling and shrieking and *displaying*. I enjoyed watching all this, though it had the collective effect of making me feel even less important than I already do, as I was being held by a few headsetted people in an area *away* from where the racks of clothes hung in clear plastic. Cathy and Rachel Zoe were allowed within the racks, but I was not, because I had been eating granola bars all morning like a child, and my hands were clearly unacceptably sticky and dangerous to the dresses! (Kidding, I would never let fashion people see me *eating*. What kind of person do you think I am?)

"Show me EVERYTHING!!!!" Rachel said in a fit of genuine excitement, as their hands fluttered, and Gurung began taking her from dress to dress on the racks. Zoe and Gurung progressed down the racks, with him explaining, her gasping and speaking with periods between all her words ("Oh. My. God. This. Is. So. Stunning. I. Can't. Even. Handle. The. Purple"). Everyone in the room acted like they weren't captivated by the exchange, but they totally were, and everyone's life at that moment revolved around it. Except maybe Cathy, who exchanged pleasantries with Rachel, though she didn't embrace her while lifting her body off the ground and so Rachel therefore didn't get the opportunity to wrap her legs around Cathy's waist. There is not a lot of *displaying* that goes with this interaction, because when two women talk it's frowned upon to act as though they're in a day care center, but when a woman and a gay man talk, years of adult development and maturation can acceptably be tossed out the window.

In a few minutes, Rachel left, as though her presence were all just a montage in someone else's reality show. At this point, I was supposed to get to talk to Prabal, but it didn't happen because the models had to put in their runway dresses! Time waits for no man! (Except at Fashion Week, when it actually waits for all of them.)

A mass of slow-moving people entered the venue a few minutes before the show started: evidence of a major celeb walking among us. All I could see of this Famous One gracing us with her presence that day was a giant curly mass of yellow-and-pink cotton candy wig topped with a pillow-sized pink iridescent bow. The dramatically accessorized hair bobbed within a circle of giant security guards and various other people looking extremely purposeful. I figured it was Nicki Minaj, though someone in the crowd loudly asked, "IS THAT LADY GAGA?" Oh, the fool, mistaking the top of Nicki Minaj's head for Lady Gaga's! In a room full of fashion people! That was so embarrassing for him! I tweeted the errant remark immediately and it got more reactions than 90 percent of my other tweets combined that Fashion Week. For that, I would like to thank, deeply, the gay community.

After Nicki Minaj was seated and everyone who had left their seats to ogle her—thereby setting back the progress we'd made toward starting the show by about 60 percent—had been forced by security to sit down again, the show finally started more than half an hour late. As annoying as this is, it doesn't really matter since fashion shows have one-hour time slots, and the shows themselves take only a few minutes. Finally, I got to see what exactly had been going on with all the colors and patterns hanging in the plastic wrap backstage.

That season, Gurung showed sheer pants dripping with purple metallic Latex, flirty dresses with mesh paneling where you'd expect to see a woman's underpants, and pretty floral-inspired prints. Some of these prints looked the way turquoise and floral wallpaper would look if you were high and stared at it too long. These things would definitely get me photographed. Too bad I was more likely to turn into a cat than be allowed to borrow them.

Everyone clapped, and Prabal came out onto the runway to receive his applause. Once the show wrapped, I got three minutes backstage to talk to the designer. Then everyone dashed off to their next show, except the people with especially good hair and expensive shoes and striking monochromatic pantsuits who decided to linger around to pose for street-style photographers while either waiting for their drivers or *pretending* to wait for their drivers so they could get attention. I would look so stupid trying to do this.

With a few days of Fashion Week left, I had nothing but the borrowed Miu Miu shoes to wear. My editor pulled me aside and got serious.

"You just have to make do with what we have," she said. "Wear a white button-down and jeans, the Miu Miu shoes, Diana's bracelets, and red lipstick. Not a brick red, but *street-style* red. I'll loan you my Chanel purse." I figured that anyone who owned her own Chanel purse knew what she was talking about. And Diana and I felt relieved we would no longer have to scramble trying to call in all the clothes on hold for J. Lo or the other Fashion Week Bambis who might need them.

I dilly-dallied about getting the assignment done because I felt nervous about *trying* to be a street-style star. I felt comfortable operating as a behind-the-scenes member of this crazy scene. I always wanted to make it as a writer and editor. If ever I were to get attention from photographers, I envisioned that it would be warranted by my hard work and success, or moving into a position that made me inherently interesting enough to photograph, like most editors in chief. And quite frankly, I didn't want to court the attention. There's a quote I like from David Sedaris about his advice to aspiring David Sedarises that perfectly captures my issues with self-promotion: "I don't think pushiness helps at all. It's unbecoming and bespeaks a talent for self-promotion rather than for writing." But marketing oneself is a vital part of the fashion industry, and you see this throughout popular fashion blogs—the most successful aren't necessarily the best, but they are expert promoters. If they weren't, they wouldn't get front-row seats at shows.

Somehow, I had gotten myself an assignment to do the exact thing I never thought I'd do. Still I had committed to getting the story, so I went home and tried to find street-style-y jeans and a stylish-enough white button-down. I grabbed a couple white shirts and a couple pairs of jeans and took them to the office the next day in a shopping bag. I had been told to style my hair wavy—you know, carefree and low maintenance like I didn't try at all. Because do not forget that the secret to being stylish is to look like you didn't try at all when you actually tried really fucking hard.

When I got to work on the appointed day, Diana and my editor examined the options and told me to wear paint-splattered boyfriend jeans that rolled up around the ankle with a crisp white shirt by +J (that's fancy for "from Uniqlo," FYI) tucked in. I rolled up the sleeves a little bit and slipped on a bunch of Diana's bangles. I looked like I was wearing a rhinestone-studded Slinky by Juicy Couture on my arm. And just in case that wasn't extreme enough (because at this stage of street style, you could wear an oversized glittery clamshell from the Victoria's Secret Fashion Show around your entire torso and you would not look overdressed), I unbuttoned the top couple of shirt buttons to reveal what you might call a "statement choker" by Dannijo that was lying around the fashion closet. I wore Diana's lipstick, slung the black quilted Chanel purse over my arm, slipped into the towering Miu Miu glitter booties, added oversized black Prada glasses that I had once found in the back of a cab, and I was ready to go. I felt like a reality TV star who got dressed for the sole purpose of cruising through paparazzi. Look out, Fashion Week—another tacky bitch is on her way!

I convinced the magazine to hire a car for me for the day, because if I was going to get photographed as much as possible I would need to be in as many places as possible as quickly as possible—without ruining my look. And, despite Fashion Week having a centralized venue referred to as "the tents" where most shows are supposed to take place, two consecutive shows on my list of things to hit were at different addresses.

Since Fashion Week wouldn't be Fashion Week if there weren't constantly a new thing that's cooler than an older thing, new venues continually crop up. Some designers show at Milk, a photo studio located in the meatpacking district, a neighborhood that's become hip to the point of self-parody. The Chihuahuas that live over there dress even tackier than the Europeans who wear black stilettos and liquid leggings to wait two hours for champagne brunch there every Saturday and Sunday. Around the corner from Milk you will also find the boutique Jeffrey, which is so absurdly Fashion it became a skit on *Saturday Night Live*.

Theoretically, when your show is not at the tents, it should be at Milk, but that's never the case because some designers, despite possessing the credentials and means to show in these places, get sponsored to show elsewhere or simply prefer something grander. Marc Jacobs shows without fail in the Lexington Avenue Armory, on the opposite side of town, because the space is gigantic and he can erect a runway within his own extravagant art installation. (For his fall 2011 show, for instance, he spent $1 million, possibly more, the *New York Times* reported, on a set that involved erecting walls of tufted vinyl, which company president Robert Duffy said, "only half-joking, was a padded cell"; the floor and benches were entirely mirrored; and each of the sixty-three models wore $180 worth of fake hair.) Alexander Wang likes to show in non–Mother Ship venues; since 2010, he has preferred the pier, usually on the very west, difficult-to-access side of Manhattan. It's possible he likes it because it looks like a big empty warehouse, and over the past eight years anyone in New York who wants to be cool makes sure a significant portion or aspect of their lives takes place in big, empty industrial spaces. The dingier and bigger and emptier the warehouse is, the cooler you are, hence the move of many hipsters from the gentrified parts of Brooklyn to the abandoned factory buildings to their east, that have no insulation in the walls, possibly no heat in the living quarters at all, and are about as comfortable to occupy in the winter as a bathtub lined with damp bedsheets. But Alexander Wang can show on his Chosen Pier that is out of everyone's way, a good distance removed from all the other shows because his clothes—the kinds of things people who live in warehouses and also have money are supposed to wear if they want to live up to their reputation of dwelling in a warehouse—have become the biggest must-sees of New York Fashion Week.

So it was not snobbery to believe mass transit was not going to work. At the tail end of summer, when Fashion Week occurs, the subway feels like a steam room in a Dumpster, and subjecting one's skin to that does not aid in looking beautiful. Also, I'd be wearing uncomfortable shoes all day and I am a *pansy* about uncomfortable shoes. Besides, being driven around all day conveys an air of signif-icance, and the most captivating street-style subjects embody this air. Given that my outfit was only mildly significant, the car was part of the costume, really.

My first show was Vera Wang—the designer famous for celebrity red carpet and wedding gowns—at the tents in Lincoln Center. This meant I would have the opportunity to sashay my ass around the large Lincoln Center plaza where photographers look for peo-ple to shoot. This particular show is attended by all the important editors of all the major fashion magazines along with a few pretty famous celebs, which brings out the whole horde of photographers.

And so commenced one of the most awkward days of my life.

If all the sparkly shit on my person and the textbook-sized Chanel bag hanging off my arm didn't make me interesting, at least my bangles jingled a lot. So when I walked I sounded like Santa: *jingle jingle jingle* ~stop~ *pose* *jingle jingle jingle jingle*.

I soon realized this outfit made it disturbingly, unexpectedly easy for me to get attention. Within a few struts around the plaza, somehow managing not to fall over in the heels, some Japanese photographers were all UP in my Juicy Couture Slinky. They wanted photos of my whole outfit but also my wrists, my shoes, my statement choker. Had they the proper imaging equipment, they probably would have X-rayed me to see what accessories my organs were wearing that day. They also wanted to know who made what—the shoes and the bag were obvious, but who made the bangles? The choker? *The white shirt?* It was frantic. But: I was doing it. *I was street style.*

When I stepped inside the tents, another small throng of photographers gathered around me, kneeling at my glitter shoes as though begging for the secret to my fabulousness. As uncomfortable as this kind of attention makes me feel when I'm thinking about getting it, it felt kind of *not that bad* to actually get it. *Is this why people become shamelessly self-promotional?* I wondered. *Because attention for something as base level in terms of achievement as wearing clothes and walking around is so addictive it's like the only thing I want to do for the rest of Fashion Week if not my life?* Multiply the attention I was receiving by about 100, and you have a day in the life of super-famous fashion blogger Susie Bubble at Fashion Week. If Susie, author of *Style Bubble*, one of the most successful fashion sites of its kind, is the Angelina Jolie of Fashion Week street style, I was like a D-list *Bachelorette*-level reality star at *least*.

After Vera Wang, I had to head downtown to West Chelsea for the Rodarte show, one of the most avant-garde of New York Fashion Week where you are pretty much guaranteed to see some truly weird shit on the runway along with a Taylor Swift–level celebrity in the audience. My plan was to meet NYmag.com's street-style photographer down the block from the show so he could photograph my outfit for the story. I found him slightly removed from where most of the street-style photographers lingered. (Now you see so many street-style photographers outside major shows that they can't just wait outside the entrance to a venue—they actually have to hustle down the block to get away from the whole crowd of them if they want any chance at capturing their own "moment" with a costumed fashion person without getting elbowed in the face by an aspiring one of them who doesn't have street-style manners.) He gave me some tips on posing. Apparently, a common famous blogger pose is to put the toe of one foot on the ground crossed behind the other. I call it the "lame flamingo." This comes in handy when people want to photograph your feet because it gives them more dimension. It's also never a bad idea to pose with one hand on the hip and one hand in the crook where your bag's strap connects to your bag. This way, people can photograph your nail art *against* your bag. That's called a "detail" shot. Nothing gets street-style fanatics off like a patterned manicure floating near some purse hardware that says "Céline."

The one thing you don't want to do is stand with your legs apart, both feet facing forward—which would be my go-to pose had I not had professionals to instruct me otherwise—which makes you look "like you just got off a horse," as one street-style photographer told me. Although I have a feeling if I *had* just dismounted a horse (as my means of transportation for the day), I'd be met with much enthusiasm.

Photographers behind my colleague from NYmag.com noticed me getting my photo taken, so as I made my way down the block toward the Rodarte show, other street-style photographers approached me. Tamu McPherson, who runs the street-style site *All the Pretty Birds* and who shoots street style for *Vogue Italia*, stopped me to take my picture. I was shocked to have drawn the interest of someone as respected as she. I did not tell her that I looked special this day due to the acumen of the girls in my office, nor did I mention I didn't actually know how to dress myself beyond jeans and T-shirts.

The inside of the show venue was sweltering. As specific as fashion people get about how things are in their lives—every plant, sock, photo, teacup, shoe rack must be *just so*—I find they are largely impervious to uncomfortable climes. Probably because in order to look *fashion* year-round, you have to disregard the whims of the weather and surrender your comfort entirely to your look. It had to have been at least 100 degrees at Rodarte, and the seats were crammed in so tightly that we were practically sitting on top of each other. While I couldn't wait to go back to having my outfit photographed outside, you could look around the room and see people like Anna Wintour and Dasha Zhukova, the pretty Russian editor of art and fashion magazine *Garage*, wearing her own mint green Miu Miu glitter booties (bitch), perched in their seats like nothing about being in that room was remotely off-putting.

Since my clothes covered most of my body and my remaining exposed surface area was covered in metal jewelry, I was drenched in sweat faster than you could say, "Please do not seat me anywhere near this wet girl." So wearing these odd outfits isn't actually easy.

After the show, we shuffled out and back onto the street where the street-style paparazzi awaited our emergence. In the 80-something-degree air, my sweat began to congeal. I walked s l o w l y past the photographers in hopes that one would stop me. But Beyoncé and Taylor Swift and everyone who was über-famous in fashion had attended the show. So I stood out not at all, even with my Chanel bag, flashy shoes, and Santa jingles. I got photographed only one time postshow from the shoulders up. I felt a little sad about this, because I thought I looked like I was obviously trying (in a not-trying way, of course). And if you obviously try and no one cares, how embarrassing is that? When you cook someone dinner, you want the person to at least say, "Yum." You don't expect a Michelin star, but some acknowledgment is nice.

Back in the comfort of the air-conditioned hired car, I took out a mirror to make sure my carefully applied street-style makeup hadn't melted off my face. It very well may have, but then somehow dried back on my face in the same arrangement I had applied it. Onward.

The next stop on my journey of attention seeking was the Marchesa show at the Plaza Hotel uptown. This is where you go to see pretty princess dresses made of sparkles that actresses will wear on red carpets during award shows. I got there very early and my feet were starting to kill in the sample Miu Miu shoes, so I set out to find a place to sit. The easiest option was the restaurant/bar area adjacent to the show space. Harvey Weinstein, the film mogul and husband of Marchesa designer Georgina Chapman, was sitting at a table on the ground floor of the restaurant, suggesting that if one were there to see and be seen, this was the spot. Tables at the Plaza are arranged like they are at a wedding: around a large open space. So it's impossible not to walk into the room without announcing your own presence, basically. I walked into the area, sunglasses still on, and I *believe* Harvey Weinstein gave me a look up and down as I did so. Apparently, despite the rejection that befell me outside Rodarte, the outfit was still working. Yet here I felt enormously out of my element. I was accustomed to seeing celebrities at parties and fashion shows and movie premieres. Those places are like zoos—you go to the zoo, you know you're going to see a lemur. But seeing a lemur *outside* the zoo is a whole different experience entirely. Seeing a celebrity in the wild provokes similar emotions, which is probably why I felt incapable of subjecting myself to the scene on the ground floor of the restaurant. Some people thrive in the face of surprise; others (me) freak out and run away. I scurried upstairs as fast as my rapidly blistering feet would take me to the bar. The bar was situated on a balcony overlooking the tables below, reserved for Weinstein and other more fabulous, limelight-occupying people. Now that I was here, with my editor's Chanel purse and everything, I figured this was the perfect time for a $19 glass of white wine. Apparently, at the Plaza, this also buys you an elaborate tray of the world's finest trail mix, which was so fancy I was afraid to eat it. Thanks to all the sweating I did at Rodarte, the wine went to my head right away. As I got tipsy in the middle of this workday and spied on the restaurant below me for Page Six–style happenings, lo, not one, but *deux* Roitfelds came in. *Mesdames* Carine Roitfeld, former French *Vogue* editor, and Her Daughter Julia Restoin Roitfeld. The Roitfelds are like the queen and Kate Middleton of street style—none of their outfits escapes celebration. I could learn from these two, who are so famous on the fashion internet for having great style they don't have to post any of their own photos to keep up interest. These are entirely self-sustaining fashion internet celebrities, and if I was going to learn anything about the art of being stylish, fabulous, and worth photographing, it was from these two.

Carine and Julia arranged themselves at a table at the perimeter of the dance floor–style opening in the furniture. Because they're *très* European, they positioned their chairs so they were facing not each other but the center of the room, as though this was not a New York City restaurant but a Parisian café where people face out from their tables instead of each other. This would afford them with a view of everyone going by. I admire the French for this—I would hide my judgment behind sunglasses, but they're just honest about how that's what they're doing. *Roitfeld lesson number one: act French to curry attention, intrigue, and envy.*

The Roitfelds talked cheerfully with their hands waving about like they were just having the best time. They ordered large plates of greens (possibly arugula, for those of you keeping track of what fashion people eat), which arrived practically instantly. *Roitfeld lesson number two: engage in animated familial bonding over matching salads.*

After each took a few bites of their twin meals, they put down their forks and dashed off to the show. *Roitfeld lesson number three: do not finish meal, because you are chic and busy.*

I had grown tipsy enough to stop being afraid of eating the trail mix before me and started picking at it. (Included in the assortment were chocolate-covered almonds. This just feels important to note because one never rolls up to a bar, orders a drink, and gets presented with gourmet chocolate-covered almonds.)

When Carine and Julia finished their meals, the model-like pair ran off lithely as if their stilettos and tight skirts were the equivalents of sneakers and track shorts. This stood in stark contrast to my inability to wear heels for a day and debilitatingly constant need to adjust everything I was wearing. *Roitfeld lesson number four: do not act like you think about your clothes.*

Having finished my glass of meal-priced wine, I slipped back down the stairs and into the show venue. Being tipsy made my feet hurt less, but my entire outfit was bothering me. My metal jewelry had adhered to my skin thanks to my mostly dried sweat, my shoes felt like they were lined with burning coals, and my makeup had congealed into a papier-mâché-like mask. *Is this how personal-style bloggers and street-style stars feel in their outfits at the shows all day?* I thought. *Like they've been mummified?*

The funny thing about my outfit is that none of my fashion show friends seemed to notice that I was dressed any differently from my usual Fashion Week wear, which had never before included recognizably designer things, more than one bracelet at a time, bright red lipstick, or shoes covered in glitter. While I felt like I was quite obviously hunting for attention, everyone I interacted with (including people who had known me for quite a while) acted like this was a perfectly normal getup. And maybe it is: we dress up in our daily lives to get photographed all the time, for Facebook and Instagram and Twitter, so the only difference for getting dressed up for Fashion Week, maybe, is that we have to think about how we look more because the resulting images, taken by other people, are out of our control.

After the Marchesa show, I walked slowly out of the venue, hoping I'd stand out more here even though socialite and ex-reality-TV-star Olivia Palermo, a petite and pretty brunette with flawless skin and unfailingly shiny hair who appeared on MTV's *The City* but was otherwise dubiously employed, was getting into her SUV just feet away from me. My feet hurt so much at this point that I was lumbering. Top street-style people glide—they do not lumber—so I stopped by the curb to rest. As I did, a photographer strode in front of me and motioned as though he wanted to take my picture. I pretended to be surprised so as not to look full of myself and assumed my lame flamingo pose. He motioned for me to scoot farther into the street. So I stepped off the curb and onto the roadway. He motioned again, so I took another step toward the middle of the street. He kept motioning, so I stepped even farther away from the curb. Now I was at the yellow line in the middle of Fifth Avenue with a wall of cars stopped at a red light at the intersection directly before me. The photographer himself was in no safe position either. After trying to photograph me standing up, he decided this was no good, and so he crouched in the middle of the street right between the row of cars and me. Here I was holding a Chanel purse, wearing open-toed boots made of glitter, standing in the middle of Fifth Avenue outside the Plaza Hotel, with nothing between the wall of New York City traffic about to barrel right at me but a photographer putting his life at risk to crouch in the middle of the road to immortalize my ensemble. All I could think about was trotting back to the sidewalk as fast as my designer sparkle booties would take me. "That's great," he said, perfectly comfortable with all of this, snapping away like it was nothing. "Hold it right there! Don't move!" And just as he got his shot, the light turned, and we scampered off the street before the cars could kill us. Once on the curb, we exchanged pleasantries. I learned he was shooting for *Marie Claire*. My photo made it onto the site, making the discomfort and awkwardness of the day and that $19 drink worth it. And most important, I had pulled off the story.

Once back in my chauffeured town car, I took off my shoes and put my feet up on the backseat. I peeled off my choker and bangles and put my hair up. My day of street-styling was over, and I was headed back to my office, feet afire with pain.

The attention was addictive, I will admit. It's the kind of validating rush you might get dancing all sexy-like at a concert or a club, and you wind up on a pedestal or the jumbotron, and you feel as though the crowd surrounding you is paying homage to your incredible cool hotness. But ultimately, once you're on that jumbotron you have to keep up appearances, otherwise you're out. And keeping up appearances is fucking exhausting. I could never be the kind of person who could: (1) dress this stylishly every day, (2) afford to dress this stylishly every day (the sum of my bag and shoes had to have been around $6,000), and (3) tolerate the discomfort of dressing like this every day. I concluded I was better off wearing my own off-trend $40 jeans and hoodie, hidden behind my cubicle half-wall or my seat in the very last row at a fashion show. Being the invisible kind of blogger has its perks, one of them being blister-free feet.

I had to put on my shoes to get from the car to the building, but once I got in the elevator, my feet hurt so much that I couldn't take it. And so I did something that I have vowed, after nights out at too many nightclubs full of drunk women, never to do: I took off my shoes in public. Standing on the cold floor of the elevator was divine. Once to my floor, I limped several steps down the hallway toward my desk before bumping into Diana.

"Jesus Christ, dude," she said, slightly horrified by how I'd washed ashore after my day.

"I can't walk," I said. "Can you call in a walker for me?"

"Definitely not till after Fashion Week," she said, coming over to relieve me of the shoes, looking concerned but mostly amused as I hobbled back to my desk. I felt like the girl clawing her way out of the TV in *The Ring*: scary, gross-looking, covered in well grime, but also powerful. It topped dragging myself out of my old Jewcy.com job with a far worse beaten-down feeling years ago. And it made me incredibly thankful to have a job that involves sitting at a desk in jeans and flats most of the time instead of having to parade about in clothing that should come with a gym membership.

A stylist and/or personal-style blogger and/or person with eight billion Instagram followers I would never be, that much was certain. Writing about them, however, was a sheer delight. And now that I knew what they were up against every day, I could approach it with newfound empathy. Which, theoretically, should help me get through Fashion Week.

· 2 ·

Trendsetters

THE TALE OF THE DESIGNER SWEATPANTS I BOUGHT
WHEN I WAS STONED

Here's a downside to dressing so close to the cutting edge that you sometimes look insane: people who exist outside the fashion world—in other words, basically everyone—won't "get" you.

Once my attempt to be Fashion, outside of my street-style experiment, almost threatened my relationship with my boyfriend.

It all began, as these things often do, at a sample sale.

A sample sale is where labels mark down unsold merchandise and sample garments—the items that get loaned out to magazine editors and hang in showrooms for buyers from stores. At a sample sale, you can get designer things not for cheap necessarily (it's not Forever 21—they're not giving it away), but you're often looking at Madewell prices. For women who work in fashion, many of whom are not born rich and don't make the mid-six-figure salaries you'd need to wear designer things all the time, the sample sale is essential. Some are quite popular: at Prada's seasonal sample sale, people line up around the block like it's the day before Thanksgiving at the airport. (Airports terrify me. The shoe removal, the four-dollar water, the gelatin-based Chinese buffets, the slow-moving lines you have to wait in for everything, and, worst of all, the need amid all this chaos to be *on time* for something. I just can't.) The anxiety feels similar at sample sales, where everyone's trying to be in the door first to get the good shoes and you often have to check your bag on arrival. For this reason, I avoid day one of most "hot" sales, and go on the last day, when they mark things down even more in an effort to get rid of them. The good thing about this strategy is that while I might miss out on some of the "better shit," I feel less guilty about spending money on the ridiculous stuff that ends up left over at these things.

One summer when I was working at the Cut, my friend James and I were sunning on the roof deck of my apartment building with my trustiest summer companion, a beach towel by the House of Deréon, Beyoncé and her mom's clothing line. (It had been sent to me as part of a "summer survival kit" that also included a Beyoncé T-shirt and a Beyoncé DVD-CD combo, making for unquestionably the best package I ever received as a member of the press.) Because I have no plans to run for political office and everyone knows books are the places to reveal these things: this was an occasion on which I smoked pot.

Soon enough, after a few puff-puff passes, we decided it was time for a treat.

"Are you thinking what I'm thinking?" I asked James.

"Jamba Juice."

And so I threw on shorts and a tank top over my bikini, and we ventured into the world.

On the train to SoHo, it hit me that Jamba Juice wasn't SoHo's sole premiere attraction this afternoon. "James! We have to go to the Alexander Wang sample sale!" I had been following the sale's progress on Racked, a shopping website that updates New Yorkers on the stock available at sample sales. If I learned anything going to his Fashion Week shows, it was that young women in New York City could be made instantly hip by owning a piece of Wang. Plus, being stoned, I knew I could handle the deep-seated shopping anxiety I would surely face otherwise.

When James and I went to the sale stoned in our beach clothes, it wasn't how it is now. Now it's like going to Fashion Week: street-style photographers congregate outside to shoot the hordes of narrow-hipped women who show up in asymmetrical black clothes and dark sunglasses and seem to always be secretly looking one another up and down, as though in competition over just existing.

No, in those days, the sale was just a bare room, racks and bins of clothes, and young fashion people hoping to find something slightly cooler than usual to wear to work.

Once we arrived, I was pretty high. It had not occurred to me that I might see people I know and work with (but see above re: high). As soon as we walked in, we saw our friend Diana, my co-worker and style sage.

"Hiii!" I said. "We were just *laying out.* That's why I'm wearing my *bathing suit.* Anything good here?"

James was already off in a zone, pilfering the racks.

"Yeah, so I'm getting this top," Diana said, "and maybe this dress—"

"*Ooh,* SWEATERS!" I got distracted and drifted toward a rack of cardigans. I pulled a silver silk-paneled cashmere one off the rack along with a knee-length blue shimmery one. I started trying them on over my clothes.

"James! Lookie! This is like a *cape!*" I looked at the prices taped to the walls. "Ooh these are each eighty dollars. I dunno . . ."

"Get it," James said with the utmost certainty. "Just get it."

James is an attractive gay Asian hipster who has legs for days and can pull off any item of clothing in the world. I've seen him roll up to dinner looking incredible in a SeaWorld windbreaker and neon pink fanny pack across his chest. I trust his advice implicitly not only because he always looks fantastic but also because, when it comes to getting dressed, we both love the unexpected, the weird. He's spontaneous and impulsive in the same way I am, and not just when it comes to five-dollar smoothie purchases.

I went back to flipping through the racks. "What are you getting?"

"I want a *onesie*," he said, again with the utmost certainty. He pulled a thermal white, fitted jumpsuit off the rack.

"*That?*" I said.

"Imma try it on," he said, moving toward a mirror on the wall. There were no fitting rooms, so he had to change in front of everyone.

He pulled this, what I can only describe as a unitard, over his feet and up his legs. It was a lot tighter than it looked on the hanger—like leggings but for the entire body.

Diana came by again.

"Oh, hey, we're leaving," she said, barely registering that James was now wearing a white cotton body stocking.

"I'm gonna get it!" James said. I, now even more high, was laughing at James uncontrollably.

"You're getting that?" she said to him, straight-faced.

"What are you going to wear it with?" I asked.

"I'm gonna dye the bottom. Dip-dye. So it looks like pants. And I'm gonna wear it out. Everywhere. In Brooklyn."

"You are going to dip-dye that onesie? Really?" I said. I am too lazy to fold my socks 99 percent of the time, much less dip-dye or DIY *anything*. I haven't made anything that's not edible for my own personal pleasure since I owned Play-Doh.

"It's easy. I'll just dip the feet in a bucket. I can do it."

"Get it anyway. It's hilarious," I said.

Once I had regained composure, I noticed we had wedged ourselves into a corner with one of the few remaining racks that was stuffed with clothing. All of it sweatpants.

"Wait, should I get . . . sweatpants?" I picked up a light blue pair and held them up to my waist.

"Hot. Yes," James said.

"Where would I wear them?"

"To work. Da club. Everywhere."

"Can I do that?" I wondered.

"*Yes*, boo. You work in fashion. You *need* Alexander Wang sweatpants," he said.

Did I really need designer sweatpants? I wanted them in the moment, that's for sure. And when I saw them on his runway in shades of pink and blue, worn by models who had either been slicked with oil or misted with water to look like they had just walked out of a steam room, I thought—all of us there thought—*That is cool*. They were a runway trend. An off-couch, real-life trend, no. A runway trend: yes. Plus, Alexander Wang became the coolest of everything cool in 2008 because he could articulate the look of a rich hipster better than the rich hipsters themselves. He proved his genius to the fashion community after he showed a whole collection styled with ripped tights in the runway show that made me realize, when I was just starting at the Cut, that I knew zero things about fashion. And then he followed it up with sweatpants, and people absolutely did not know what to do with themselves. Maybe it was just exciting for the coolest designer in New York to give us permission to wear comfortable bottoms. Elastic waistbands. *Eating* clothes. Or maybe he was just fucking with us to see if we'd go for it.

I bought them without trying them on. They were $50. Fifty-dollar sweatpants.

They had a drop crotch, drawstring waist, and asymmetrical pockets halfway down the thigh. They tapered at the ankle, and I decided the best way to wear them was scrunched up around my calves.

I wore the pants to work and to parties, but never just to lounge around the house. As a member of the very small club that took the sweatpants trend seriously, I felt *soooo* cool. *I work in fashion, and I have Alexander Wang sweatpants*, I would think when I had them on. *I am cool.*

Note that never in the history of humanity have sweatpants been the thing that defined any cool person's coolness. But this is what happens when you buy things at sample sales when you're high.

I can never go to the Alexander Wang sale without buying something strange. I went once after I bought the sweatpants and left with a sleeveless mock-turtleneck cropped sweater and a jean mom skirt with crooked silver paint running up and down the sides. If it weren't for that paint—which later started peeling, making it look unfortunately blistered—it would just be your average knee-length denim skirt for the kind of woman who wears Tevas and her husband's old sweaters. But when I decided to buy those things, all I could think about was owning yet another piece of Alexander Wang, and Carine Roitfeld, the former French *Vogue* editor, who once was shot by street-style bloggers wearing a denim mom pencil skirt.

I will get this skirt and look so street style at the next Fashion Week, I thought.

A professional stylist later suggested I divest my wardrobe of said skirt.

. . .

Since working in fashion, I have acquired and worn a slew of things that are objectively ridiculous. Pink acid-wash shorts. Slacks with a crotch that hangs past my knees. A sweatshirt bearing a sequined tiger face. A fedora. I blame this on several things. One is impulse. The other is shopping with other fashion-oriented people. They love clothes that they haven't seen before, or clothes that haven't been popular during your lifetime, which is for some reason often equally exciting in a way your mother's closet never was.

When you leave the house in a trendy item, you won't know how people will react to you or how you'll feel wearing it. This is exciting the way vacations to new places are exciting. You don't know what awaits you around each turn! Will there be a woman who looks at you in envy? A tourist who looks up from his map to gawk like you're something he's never seen before? Whatever it is, it's all attention.

Things you "shouldn't" buy are known as trendy. Trend items are a "waste of money" because they'll go out of style in a season. However, trend items are hands-down the most fun things to wear because, while everyone has a T-shirt, not everyone has a leather turtleneck crop top. And what fun is wearing a T-shirt when you could be wearing a leather crop top? No fun, that's what. You know what else is no fun? Looking like everyone else. No one understands this better than stage divas—that's why they always wear different outfits from their backup dancers. So it is with trends: you can either blend into the background wearing what everyone is wearing, or you can take a risk, be your own woman, and be stared at. It's like I always say: better to elicit a negative reaction than to elicit *no* reaction. Everyone wears jeans to restaurants, but not everyone wears *sweatpants* to restaurants. Being different like this is to live at the pinnacle of trendiness. And to exist at the pinnacle of trendiness, while a surefire way to get photographed a lot at Fashion Week, will perplex your friends and family who don't work in fashion.

As I've stated, style doesn't come naturally to me. I had to learn it the way I did math. Enablers—like James—helped me spend money I "shouldn't" have spent on things I "shouldn't" have bought. Enablers can be thought of as instructors in advanced placement courses—there to teach you the calculus proofs of getting dressed—and they really helped me break out of my safe place of jeans and T-shirts.

Once when I was "on a break" from a boyfriend, my friend Chris—another enabler—took me shopping. When I am upset, I buy things to cheer myself up. Probably 50 percent of the things I don't need were acquired as a means of making myself feel better about my life. Impulse shopping somehow delivers the same emotional benefit as going out and grabbing a drink after a rough day—and research shows it has the same temporary effect of mood boosting—except it tends to cost more. (Exceptions run rife, of course: New York never met a $17 cocktail it didn't like.) At this time, I was so upset about the guy, I was ready to spend any amount of money to make my feelings hurt less.

Chris is a graphic designer who has a side business selling T-shirts and pillowcases emblazoned with Warhol-esque images of pop culture and fashion icons like Princess Diana and Britney Spears. He wears everything from tight all-black outfits to baggy Vivienne Westwood jeans tucked into those puffy blue-and-white sneakers that look like marshmallows. Accent jewelry is, remarkably, his friend. He lives in one of Brooklyn's most hipster neighborhoods and brings a Missoni towel to the beach. Practicality is not high on his list of concerns. He is an impeccable shopping partner because he always suggests things for me that I wouldn't consider for myself otherwise.

As soon as we walked into American Apparel, I went to the section I always hit first: lamé. I am drawn to shiny things. This must be one of those traits that goes back to evolution—you know, cavelady survival strategies. How much easier would it be to get the hottest caveman's attention in gold lamé leggings and a shiny purple leotard than some drab old buffalo skin? I believe this principle still holds. Pop stars wouldn't be the attention magnets they are if they weren't shiny.

"*Ooooh, shinyyyy,*" I cooed over the racks. "Should I get something shiny? I'm so depressed."

"Um, no." Thankfully, Chris dismissed my lamé longings. "You should try this on." He held up a short dark red T-shirt dress with zipper detailing on the sleeves.

"I don't know; that's too short," I said.

"Just try it on! It'll look really good on you."

I agreed, because no woman can resist the urging of a gay man who wants to see how she looks in something.

When I came out, Chris looked me up and down.

"You have to get that," he said.

The dress was so short that I'd never be able to wear it without tights. But he was right: this dress made me look good. And nothing I ever picked out for myself ever made me look good.

"Wear that when you see him. You'll get back together," Chris said.

"It's sixty-five dollars, though," I pointed out.

"Just get it. You only live once. You'll look back on your early twenties and regret not buying that and all the shortest, tightest dresses you can find. Trust."

I wore the red American Apparel dress to see the guy. Chris was right: we got back together.

. . .

There are two kinds of people in this world: those who wear leather pants and those who do not. You probably wouldn't own leather pants unless you had a place to wear them. Like a casino in Europe. Or Fashion Week.

That is because trends are environment-driven. Of course, the people working in the fashion industry wear the weirdest-looking stuff—they exist in a hot tub of eccentricity where material personal effects are what most immediately separates them from Not Them. Having spent a number of years in fashion media by this point, I own and wear leather pants now. Once I started working for Cosmopolitan.com in the Hearst Tower—which also houses the employees of *Elle* and *Harper's Bazaar*—it seemed like a non-option. Leather pants are to the Hearst building what cowboy hats are to Montana: a part of the landscape.

You might think we have fashion designers to thank/blame for the nonsensical apparel that people can pull off only in the presence of other fashion people. It's true: we do have fashion designers to thank/blame for the trends that trickle down to fast fashion stores like Forever 21 and Zara, where everyone shops and everyone can be made to look like a dumpier version of a fashion show model. A few designers, like Marc Jacobs and Miuccia Prada, hold such outsize influence that whatever they show one season everyone copies the next. When Marc Jacobs puts models in Amish shoes, and everyone declares him a genius, I smile and nod the way I would when someone shows me photos of their baby. I can understand that this means a great deal to the parent and other people in that parent's inner circle, but I cannot—will not—ever "get" it. Other people's baby photos are just never going to mean the same thing to me as they do to people who just like babies. The same goes for most fashion. If it did, I'd be Carine Roitfeld. She is a magical fashion-world nymph who makes humans feel embarrassed to be human. I am the girl who makes other people feel better about themselves by existing.

The truth is, there is an even Higher Power than fashion designers. They are called *trend forecasters*, and they are the weather people of fashion. While the weather people check climate trends, wind patterns, ocean currents, and so forth, trend forecasters monitor the length of our hemlines and the height of our heels. They predict the dress of everyone everywhere, and no one even realizes it. Walk by Ann Taylor and see what's in the window. Pass through a grocery store checkout line and see the latest red carpet fashions to make the covers of the tabloids. These are, at their core, the results of the decisions made by trend forecasters.

Chris, one of my primary enablers, is a devotee of the world's premiere trend forecaster Li Edelkoort. Every time he talks about her, it's like he's just seen a real-life centaur. Because she's that magical. All she has to do to influence what cosmetics and fashion companies sell is say words like *moss*, *nomad*, *yurt* in a seminar, and then every fast fashion store ends up with a post-apocalyptic earth mother look that leads to all of us wearing Teva knockoffs and burlap crop tops for a whole season. On the upside, in addition to the comfortable shoes, we'll save time combing our hair.

Edelkoort is paid to give lectures to employees of the world's biggest brands that make everything from makeup to clothes to cars. She tells them the current mood of culture and where that mood is going in two years' time, and they use her predictions to inform their own creative work.

Chris took me to one of her seminars held at the School of Visual Arts in New York. It felt like going to a planetarium show but about fashion and beauty trends instead of constellations. And, because this is obviously more glamorous, instead of a pamphlet, they give you a bottle of Smart Water and a square of 77 percent cacao rose-salt-and-lemon-flavored chocolate.

Edelkoort is soft-spoken and wore a black dress over pants in a way only someone who works at an art school can pull off. She began the session with a brief *affirmation* of her previous predictions, confirming that the trends she said would trend did in fact become a Thing on the runways at Fashion Week. Her presentations consist of single words followed by slides of gorgeous, impeccably curated images to illustrate her point. "Draped" was one trend, visible in a Phillip Lim sandal and a Marios Schwab gown. "Layered" followed—"another obsession," Edelkoort said. "Very poetic." Then came "frilled," aka a shit ton of ruffles, which, Edelkoort explained, "means society at large is moving up again."

She then forecasted trends that will appear nearly two years from now. The overarching theme of this collection? "Vanities," she called it. This is her polite, artistic way of saying that assholes who take endless photos of themselves on social media are not going anywhere any time soon. Ignore them at your own peril, retailers.

"One morning on the beach in Morocco, I saw a girl. She had been running, and she wanted to take a selfie of herself," Edelkoort said. "So she checked out the sea and she made a beautiful photo, me and the sea."

She continued, "We are in this crazy, crazy moment where people are creating myths of themselves. They are making their lives into larger-than-life events."

She described the archetypes of this season in, appropriately, mythic terms: the elf, sylph, and oracle were those she included in this "vanities" forecast. Others included: mermaid, Cleopatra, twins.

Edelkoort crafts a story for each of her archetypes, making the seminar like story time for adult fashion people. Mermaid, for example, isn't just indicative of blue and sequins, but rather "young women who go to bars at night beautifully dressed . . . tease the guys, have them buy all the drinks for the girls, and then they just leave them," she explained. "They're very nasty. I think men are getting almost afraid of them."

The druid, a "darker story," was inspired by "pagan cults of the Celtic Druids," who, according to the booklet Edelkoort provided seminar attendees that explained all of these archetypes, predicted the future through bird flight and song and dwelled in the forest. "You look at the forest in the afternoon, it's shadow and light. It's using linens, it's using barklike materials." The fashion-world druid of 2016 would invoke "magical, mystical, couture fabrics," Edelkoort explained, including dark greens in yarn and lace paired with other shades of green and purple. Picture a princess who might have lived in a tree in the forest of your favorite '90s computer game Myst.

"It's sort of like an ecological punk; it's a very good direction here," Edelkoort continued. "Sort of eco-warriors. I think that the world wants to go there."

Over the course of the half-day seminar, Edelkoort told the room to stop making perfumes that smell like cake. She advised clothing makers to sell only a single garment in their stores (mono-shopping). She proclaimed that hair is the new textile for both women and men. She lingered on a photo of a man with a bushy beard with flowers and leaves growing out of it to prove her point.

After the seminar, art directors and marketers from MAC Cosmetics, Banana Republic, and many other businesses would return to their offices and create campaigns and mood boards with Edelkoort's recommendations in mind. And this is how your "going out" wardrobe ends up consisting of blue sequins in two years. This high-level, profound, art-world reading of society is how a trend becomes a trend.

I often forget that these kinds of conversations about Fashion happen only within the industry. The fashion world is such a bubble that it's hard to remember what's on the outside, even when you do sit in the back row. And what's on the outside is a whole lot of people who see sweatpants as an item to be worn secretly in one's own home. I was reminded, some months into my relationship with my boyfriend, Rick, that he and his parents were just those kinds of people when he invited me to dinner with his dad and stepmother. I had met his dad previously on a weekend trip to the beach, so I technically knew him, but not well—definitely not well enough for him to understand why I'd own and wear designer sweatpants.

It was gorgeous out—sunny but not hot—so I threw on the sweatpants, a white tank top, a silver cuff bracelet, and black high-heeled sandals. I thought I looked completely fabulous—casual yet dressy, cool yet not try-hard, hipster yet not obnoxious.

I arrived at Rick's Tribeca apartment where he was hanging out with his dad and stepmom. He wore khakis with a dress shirt tucked in and loafers. His dad was similarly dressed, and his stepmom wore the de facto elegant mom uniform of a slightly drapey but still figure-flattering top and nicely cut trousers with a shiny pendant necklace. (Once women reach a certain age, I've noticed, they love nothing more than a giant necklace. I fully expect to turn forty-five with a hubcap hanging from a chain around my neck.)

"Hey, sweetie," Rick said. "You remember my dad, and this is Lorri."

After a few seconds of smiling at each other, Rick's brow furrowed in a way that can only suggest something was very, very awkward.

"What are you wearing?" he said.

"What? Alexander Wang?"

"Sweatpants?"

"Oh, they're *on-trend*."

His dad and stepmom looked on with nervous smiles.

We walked across the street to City Hall Grill. It's the kind of place where if you went during lunch on a Tuesday, you'd be surrounded by businessmen wearing suits. On the weekends, you get families wearing polo shirts and boat shoes. We ordered a tower of cold shellfish. I had a margarita in a tall, skinny glass. Rick's stepmom showed me her sparkly pendant necklace up close. Everyone enthused over the steak.

Everything was going great, I thought. As soon as the meal ended, Rick's dad would pull him aside and tell him how bright and funny and good at dinner conversation I am and order him to marry me immediately.

After we walked his dad and stepmom to their car, we returned to Rick's apartment.

"Sweatpants?" he said again.

"I have heels on!" I protested.

"To a nice restaurant?"

"Babe, this is New York. Everyone's wearing sweatpants now."

Rick is a man of few words and reveals his truest feelings only when pressed.

Well, not long thereafter, he was pressed. We were in the middle of one of our first fights on the phone. He was arguing that I didn't try hard enough with his family and friends.

I was outraged! I tried *so hard* with his family and friends. I began listing all that I had accomplished with his family and friends over the six or so months we had been together.

"You wore sweatpants to dinner," he blurted out.

Gasp! I couldn't believe I was having a fight with a man over how I was dressing. I would never be with a person who told me what to wear. I am a child of the postfeminist generation and I dress for myself—not for a boyfriend, and certainly not a boyfriend's dad. Trends are fun and not meant to be taken seriously. This would certainly not be the last strange thing I wore. I cried into the phone for a little bit.

"Omigod," I began. "Did your dad . . . *say something?*"

"Yes! You wore sweatpants! To dinner! At a nice restaurant!"

"But I wore *heels!*" I said.

"My dad couldn't believe you wore sweatpants. It's really disrespectful."

I had spent a long time thinking about what to wear because I always spend an inordinate amount of time thinking about what to wear. You could scrub and demildew an entire shower in the time it takes me to pick out most of my outfits. *The sweatpants were a carefully considered choice representative of my increasingly urgent need to be Fashion. Why couldn't he see that?* Rick should have been happy with my sweatpants. They were the opposite of the blue-sequined mermaid attire Edelkoort described. If my outfit suggested anything according to profound art-world trend-forecaster assessment, it was that I was the opposite of those evil mermaids.

. . .

Rick and I made up. Many outfits later, we got engaged and married. Rick tells me he knows better now than to comment on my clothes. I have learned to take his feedback on my apparel into consideration when we have to penetrate his world deeply or go to a bagel brunch with his family. Now that I've gotten my youthful, impulsive sweatpants-buying out of my system, I concentrate more on accruing clothes that are fun but perhaps slightly easier for people who have never been to Fashion Week to understand. Fortunately, the two weeks out of the year that Fashion Week occurs allow me to wear all the ridiculous outfits I'd want to wear in a year anyway. The beauty of the fashion industry is that while everyone in it judges everyone, in a way, they also judge no one.

The sweatpants and I are still together, but only on days when I'm lounging around my apartment and it's cold outside, because they have a little bleach stain on the front now. I don't know how it got there but somehow that made them seem unfit for nice dinners. Besides, the sweatpants that are now in style have a much slimmer fit. And no one wants to be off-trend in *old* sweats.

Now that Rick and I live together, every time I wear the pants I'm all, "Remember *these* pants? [*wink wink*]"

He'll sort of grin and we'll have a laugh over the whole thing. I even joke about it with his dad now.

However, I did learn a valuable lesson from the whole experience: don't ever go shopping high. Drunk shopping is fine. Stoned shopping will never end well.

· 3 ·

Designers

WHEN RACHEL ZOE SENT ME A TREE

A couple years into my job at *New York* mag, I was just minding my own business, doing the usual—sitting at my desk, staring at my screen—when the phone rang.

"This is Amy," I said. I expected to be greeted by a publicist asking if I read her press release about this one tank top Kate Bosworth wore when she was walking to her car.

Instead: "I have Carrie for you," said the unmistakably scared voice of someone who makes a living by dialing phones for someone who is more powerful. Now I was getting scared. I felt like I was about to have the post-Pap-smear conversation no woman wants to have with her gynecologist. (I have checked with my friends in the business, and they have confirmed that they, too, view many publicists with the same affection as those who probe our vaginas with cold metal instruments.)

Carrie? I thought. *Do I know a Carrie?* Truthfully, the only "Carrie" ringing bells upstairs was the fictional character with the last name "Bradshaw." Was this a magical daydream where she materializes as a real person to rescue me from my cubicle and take me on a walk around the West Village while we wear belts under our boobs and tutus on our heads?

No.

"Amy. It's Carrie." I couldn't help but wonder: *Do I know a Carrie who is important enough to employ an assistant who shoulders the extreme burden of pressing buttons on a phone?* And more importantly: *How do I get one so I can screen calls like this and generally avoid doing things for myself?*

It is a universal truth of working in fashion/glossy media that everyone wants an assistant. Assistants are status symbols, like Chanel bags. Could you get by without one? In many cases, yes. But why would you if you could afford it? Assistants, like the Right Purses, automatically make a person seem four times as important and powerful as they are. But most importantly, assistants allow their bosses to avoid interactions with people. Assistants act as a buffer between you and your phone calls, you and your email, you and your nearest Starbucks, all of which can be filled with mightily unpleasant things like incompetency and waiting. And, worst of all, people you don't want to talk to.

"Are you writing a story about Rachel Zoe?" Carrie demanded. I felt like I had done something very, very wrong. She sounded as though she had just found out that I had slept with her husband.

"So-and-so from Bloomingdale's said you're writing a story about Rachel. Are you writing a story about Rachel?"

Ohhhh, so this Carrie was Rachel's *publicist.* I started to get this feeling I had in grade school after I got in trouble for telling another girl in the periphery of my social circle the ghost story about Bloody Mary. I obviously *had* to tell this girl, Colleen, because this was third grade, and if you weren't "in the know" about the ghost story going viral across campus, you were obviously setting yourself up to be some kind of loser. Anyway, I related that if she turned off the lights and performed some kind of ritual, like saying "Bloody Mary" a few times while turning around or something, she'd be faced with a lady named "Mary" covered in blood in the mirror. Well, Colleen took the tale a little too seriously, and one day her mom accosted me in the middle of an assembly wanting to know why I made her daughter afraid to go to the bathroom, as though *this had been my plan all along*. I wanted to say, "Your daughter is a moron for being afraid of using the toilet because of *ghosts*." But I couldn't say that because I was the child and the mom was a *mom*— the *adult*—which made me the Lesser Person in the situation, unable to explain that I was actually doing poor Colleen a favor. I have precisely that feeling just about every time I talk to publicists. Even if they're just saying "Hello!" I automatically feel like I need an excuse for my existence.

"Yes, I just interviewed so-and-so from Bloomingdale's yesterday," I began. "See, I'm writing a story about Rachel's new clothing line. I thought it was just *incredible* that she's launched her first collection in *so many stores*. And I'm working on a story about how unusual and *fabulous* that is."

"Is this going to be a snarky, nasty story?"

How is she inside my brain? I tended to approach stories from a cynical point of view at this point in my career, but that's because I was writing on the internet when "bloggers" were all known for being snarky and "blogging" was still like this nouveau thing that people like my dad didn't really believe was an actual job.

I got in trouble for being "mean" from time to time at the Cut. I only had to apologize for it once, and that was when I wrote about the phenomenon that is haul vlogging. Haul vlogging, for those of you blessedly unfamiliar, is when you go shopping, come home, sit down in front of your web cam, and make a video of yourself talking about the things you bought. Let me tell you, more thrilling developments have not been made in the world of YouTube entertainment, no they have not. People haul vlog everything from Claire's jewelry to—and quite famously—Yankee Candles. I decided to do a post on haul vlogging one day, so I found what I thought was a particularly vapid example for a post. I combined it with a paragraph of text about what haul vlogging is, adding that people who haul vlog need lives and possibly cats. (I can defend the latter comment by affirming that I believe every person in the world needs a cat. Cats are the whipped cream and cherry of home life. They just are. I love them.)

Unbeknownst to me, this person had a huge following online, which quickly rallied behind her. They left hundreds of comments in support of her under my post. They called me a bitch. They called me fat. They called me ugly.

They attacked me on Twitter, too, which only served to increase my following, which meant that my self-esteem netted neither gain nor loss when the whole thing ended. However, the serious downside was that all the comments from this vlogger's followers shot the post to the top of the most-commented-on and most-viewed lists on the site, which everyone saw as soon as they landed on the homepage. These were usually an indicator of which bloggers won the website that day. However, in this instance, it meant that I had lost the website hard enough for my boss to call me on a weekend and tell me that I had to write an apology post. I wrote the apology post the next day. The comments from our regular Cut readers said things like, "Oh, Amy, you caved." Even though I had expressed a commonly held opinion about a ridiculous activity, I had made the mistake of coming out and expressing that opinion much too bluntly. But would I have told this girl to her face that she needed a life and a cat? No, which is why it was a mistake to put it in writing.

I quickly learned that fashion bloggers have to be really careful not to offend people. If you say something like, "[Insert Italian designer here] resembled orange Fanta in his swim trunks as the yacht pulled into port under a searing Mediterranean sun," and that Italian designer gets really upset at having just been likened to orange soda by some rando sitting in a cubicle halfway around the world, his label might very well threaten to pull ads. Then you'll get into trouble. And you can forget owning your own yacht (*obviously* an attainable dream on a blogger's salary) because that Italian designer, Fanta colored or not, is funding your paycheck. It is thanks to that designer, that orange yacht owner with all the money, that you get the opportunity to sit in that cubicle and make jokes about ironic T-shirts. I also figured out that I couldn't randomly skewer a lot of the people involved in the industry without reason because I might want to interview them one day.

You know, like Rachel Zoe.

"*Nooooo*. No, not at *all*," I reassured Carrie. "Everyone's talking about how Rachel's line is so amazing, and everyone wants to wear it, and how she has *such* a strong vision." This wasn't a lie—Zoe had just launched a clothing line that had been picked up by Bloomingdale's, Bergdorf Goodman, Neiman Marcus, and Nordstrom, among others. For a first-time designer (meaning, if you don't count her QVC collections), this was an undeniably unbelievable debut.

"And you weren't even going to *tell* Rachel you were doing this story?"

Writers don't *have* to tell designers they're writing about them. If they did, blogs wouldn't exist.

But if you want the designer's involvement with something, you have to go to their protectors eventually to get them to talk to you. I assumed Rachel wouldn't talk to me anyway since I tended to treat her with the same amount of skepticism on the blog as I did Miss Universe evening wear. Though I planned to ask her for comment after I figured out whether or not retailers were actually into her clothes or just viewed carrying them like going to other people's weddings—an obligation.

"I was going to *tell* Rachel, yes," I said to Carrie. "I was just doing some initial reporting and hadn't gotten around to reaching out to you guys yet! You were next on my list. For *sure*."

"All right," she said, sounding a lot less like she wanted to punch me in the face. "I'll see if Rachel can talk to you."

"Thank you! This story will be *so* great"—and the phone clicked.

For magazines like *Vogue*, access to famous designers is probably pretty easy most of the time. *Vogue* hardly ever writes anything bad about designers (or anyone else, for that matter). This also helps with advertising, allowing Anna Wintour to beef up her prized September issue with ad pages, so she can truck the thing into her meeting with Condé Nast executives on a wheelie cart, and then go on TV and talk about how much the issue WEIGHS and gloat about HOW FAT her magazine is this September (fatter than ever!). It is truly the only celebration of fatness the industry throws all year, for those September issues.

That's how you *avoid* getting "banned." Innocuous things can get you "banned," and once you are "banned," you have to work to get the ban "lifted." This is how designers hold sway over coverage: they threaten to ban outlets from their shows and pull advertising if outlets displease them.

Getting banned feels much easier to do. You might make some fairly innocuous observations about the attendees at a designer's show, as *New York Times* critic Cathy Horyn did once, prompting a ban letter from Armani, which she turned into an article about how she doesn't really need to go to his show anyway since all the runway photos just end up online. "What being banned tells me is that fashion has entered a borderland between the old and the new," she wrote. "Practiced mainly by older designers, whose careers took flight in the 1980s, banning seems a reflexive action against a perceived threat to their power."

Though *Vogue* possesses the uncanny ability to not get banned, even it was in fact banned from one designer's show—Azzedine Alaia—because it never photographs his clothing, presumably partly because he doesn't advertise and business-wise it has no reason to cater to him. (Fashion magazines tend to photograph the clothing of their advertisers.) Once an alleged list of whose clothes had to be photographed the most for a *Harper's Bazaar* shoot leaked on the internet. It read:

MINIMAL
10 PAGES +1A
PHOTOGRAPHER: [REDACTED]
FASHION EDITOR: [REDACTED]
LOCATION: LA

IN PRIORITY ORDER:
1-GIORGIO ARMANI
2-MICHAEL KORS
3-CALVIN KLEIN
4-YSL
5-CHLOÉ
6-VERSACE
7-AKRIS
8-DEREK LAM
9-CAROLINA HERRERA
10-CÉLINE
11-GIVENCHY (CHECKING)
12-STELLA MCCARTNEY
13-HERMÈS
14-REED KRAKOFF
NON-ADVERTISER (IN ALPHABETICAL ORDER)
1-3.1 PHILLIP LIM
2-HELMUT LANG
3-NARCISO RODRIGUEZ
4-PRABAL GURUNG
5-PROENZA SCHOULER

This was greatly scandalous, as though *no one knew this happened.*
(We do.) And I doubt that many readers care that small, penniless
avant-garde labels that make hats out of Slinkies aren't getting photographed by *Harper's Bazaar* as regularly as Michael Kors. French
Vogue and all its staff was also once banned from Balenciaga for a
variety of rumored reasons, one involving an editor taking a sample Balenciaga coat to Max Mara, a label she consulted for. Eventually, the editor of the magazine had tea with Balenciaga's designer

and patched things up before going to ride on Ferris wheels together in a montage-worthy celebration of their friendship. (Kidding about everything after "tea," but I just like imagining fashion people's lives as a series of montages set to the Beach Boys hit "Wouldn't It Be Nice.")

You're surely dying to know if I've ever been banned from something. Well, yes, I have been banned from some things! And received a few threats about being banned from other things, all for similarly silly reasons, but I do love when a good ban threat letter comes through. Here's a sample.

Hi Amy,

I have to say I was greatly saddened to see that you chose to include [REDACTED DESIGNER]'s name in the article you ran today on the Cut headlined "[REDACTED]."

[BOSS OF LETTER WRITER, REDACTED] is personally quite upset about your continued insistence on reporting a rumor that is not only yesterday's news, but has been denied multiple times by [REDACTED LABEL] and its parent corporation [REDACTED]. [CEO OF REDACTED COMPANY] . . . has been quoted in WWD as strictly denying the rumors that [REDACTED DESIGNER] was at all in risk of losing his job. Quite on the contrary, he invited [REDACTED DESIGNER] to [REDACTED PARENT COMPANY]'s financial results meeting and credited him with helping turn [REDACTED LABEL] around. The New York Times also ran an article recently completely denying the rumors.

In continuing to spread these baseless rumors, you are not only practicing bad journalism, but you are offending [REDACTED CEO] personally, and [REDACTED PARENT COMPANY] as a company. Additionally, to mention [REDACTED DESIGNER]'s name in any

capacity in an article that is about substance abuse, drugs, etc., is
further unfair and unnecessary defamation of his character.

    There is absolutely no truth to these claims. Should these sort of
articles continue to run on NYMag.com, [REDACTED BOSS OF
LETTER WRITER] has vowed to make it his personal mission to not
only exclude New York magazine from all [REDACTED PR FIRM]'s
news and events, but also to make sure that [REDACTED PARENT
COMPANY] & [REDACTED PARENT COMPANY'S CEO] are made
specifically aware of the poor journalism practices taken by NY Mag
as an organization.

               I hope you can understand our frustration,
               [REDACTED]

Fun! Right? I also got into some trouble with a designer after I did a blog post foreshadowing what we *might* see in his show. He and his company president freaked out and threatened to ban the whole magazine, which had nothing to do with my blog post, from all their shows—because we were excited enough about his fashion show to even bother uncovering that he might have socks and low heels on the runway. We (but mostly *me*, who knew a model walking in the show) are such bad, bad people. I haven't been invited back since.

. . .

Famous fashion people are like Tootsie Pops. On the outside is a hard shell composed of publicists and assistants and those publicists' publicists and assistants, and it's only through much persistence and considerable work that you'll get to the human core at the center of it all. Considering Rachel's history, I can see why her Fortress of Protection is more like a jawbreaker that maybe, if you're lucky, has gum inside. First, she has, like, *double* the celebrity cred of most famous fashion people, being at once a fashion person (first stylist, then designer) and famous in her own right. She entered the tabloids as a villainlike character once everyone found out *she* was responsible for making Nicole Richie look like a beautiful, elegant, slim Los Angeles fairy princess instead of the person she used to be when she was Paris Hilton's sidekick, and dressed as though all her clothes came from mall kiosks and she lived in a Las Vegas pool. I don't know why making Nicole Richie an iconic person of style turned Rachel Zoe into an object of tabloid hatred. I think everyone was just jealous that once Rachel came into Nicole's life, she suddenly had baby-smooth J. Lo skin, lost weight, and could wear a hippie scarf as a dress and look completely spectacular. If there's anything people—especially LA people—wanted in the early 2000s it was J. Lo's skin and a certain bohemian *je ne sais quoi*. Even if that certain *je ne sais quoi* is purely derived from people forgetting your hair used to be two colors: brunette and bleached. Anyway, you can see why Rachel would be wary of reporters. Her good work in La La Land transforming hopeless celebrities into people who had the strength to just say no to denim shorts cut off at both the waistband and leg holes was making everyone spiteful.

It's not always necessary to go through a major fashion person's hard shell. There is a highly scientific method I use to avoid this very thing, which I have practiced and perfected over the years: it's called "stalking."

This is not to be confused with the scary, can-get-you-arrested kind of stalking, like where Miranda Kerr gets home and—surprise!—you're in her kitchen smelling her washcloth and jerking off to her family portrait. Legal stalking can be done by any member of the media with an email in-box.

There are two steps to legal stalking: Step 1. Pay attention to boldfaced names publicists claim will attend the events they are constantly inviting you to. Resist the impulse to delete the invites for things as silly as teatime in honor of Charmin toilet paper and the cat fashion show for Meow Mix. You never know what famous persons will show up to these things, slightly drunk and willing to run their mouths. Step 2. Once you have identified your targets, show up to those places and accost them with a recording device. Without this method, I would have never come face to face with one of the most important designers of our time, Karl Lagerfeld. Long before I got that call from Rachel's publicist, when I had just started at the Cut, I received a fateful invitation for face time with his fashion majesty.

It read:

Peter MacGill

and

Gerhard Steidl

invite you to the launch of the book

KARL LAGERFELD
METAMORPHOSES of an AMERICAN
A CYCLE OF YOUTH 2003 – 2008

Reception

Friday, May 16, 2008
7:00 – 9:00 pm

And underneath all that, in the tiniest font on the whole invite, completely without ceremony or exclamation points (or any correct punctuation at all, because I guess that was out this season) or the big glittery arrow it surely deserved, was this:

KARL LAGERFELD WILL BE PRESENT

Now, when someone as famous and unusual as Karl Lagerfeld—who basically lives in a bubble where his eccentricity is heralded as genius—swings through town, you go, and you do not think twice about what else you could be doing. Especially when all else you'd be doing is drinking at one of many nightclubs where both the male and female patrons wear the exact same jeweled belts.

A bit of background on Karl: Karl is important to the world because he's created fashion that mixes the classics with camp, most famously for the house of Chanel, which people said was a lost cause when Karl took it over. He not only revived the label by making it feel luxurious, sexy, and exciting in the early '80s, but he also turned it into something that tween starlets were just as hungry to wear as people like Anna Wintour. Pause to consider how remarkable this is: can you think of a single place where you, your mom, and your grandma all want to shop, aside from the grocery store?

Karl Lagerfeld is important to me because, as one of the fanciest people on the planet—who lives as though his life were one long black-and-white Fellini movie—he is an endless study in fascination and amusement. He has said he owns "hundreds" of iPods and has been thought to employ a "nanny" to upload music to them, would rather fax than use a cell phone, and wears kimonos during overseas flights. He is also obsessed with his cat Choupette, who eats fresh seafood off fine china and has been on the cover of German *Vogue*. He goes everywhere wearing a full three-piece suit with a tie, layered silver necklaces, and the occasional diamanté brooch. He is never without fingerless leather gloves and sunglasses, and keeps his powder-white hair in a low ponytail. His look is best summed up as a cross between the Founding Fathers and Michael Jackson.

No matter what he does, he's heralded as a genius and promptly copied by nearly every other important designer. Karl's runway shows have included purses fashioned from hula hoops, full-fur Chewbacca suits, and skirt suits with beaver tails. He has that rare ability to make rich people lust for seemingly terrible things, like clogs, fur boots, and basket-weave purses. This is a very hard thing to do, but also really important for a fashion designer because what's *amazeballs* one decade is highly questionable the next (see: fringed vests for men, overalls with a strap down, brown carpets people had in their homes in the '70s). If designers never convinced us to want the things we didn't already have, we'd never shop. The next time you want something impractical you know you shouldn't buy, like pilgrim shoes, you can probably trace the influence back to someone like Karl, Marc Jacobs, and—if what you're eyeing are really tight pants and you are a man—Hedi Slimane.

Karl's theatrical spirit makes him a natural for putting on fashion shows. (I have never been invited to one because I am not important enough to attend, being neither Posh Spice, a socialite with a *Vogue* column, an Olsen twin, nor J. Lo's child.) For the purpose of dressing ladies in clothes and having them walk back and forth, he's created a faux "airplane," where the aisle served as the runway, a barn floored with hay and dirt, an iceberg imported from Northern Europe, and a carousel made from oversized Chanel purses. If

Karl ever finds himself bankrupt and without a job in fashion, I'm quite convinced he could make a career out of creating amusement parks for older, rich ladies for whom the word *summer* is primarily a verb. He could charge $200 an hour, and one of the "rides" could involve sitting in the cabin of a private plane while flight attendants serve you low-cal fish mousse. Now, would spendy fifty-year-old broads be into that or what?

One of my other favorite fun facts about Karl: he published a diet book with the least useful recipes in history, such as fish soufflé, vegetables in aspic, and ham and raspberry mousse. Naturally, it worked fabulously for him and utterly failed for everyone else who would rather not eat than either try to prepare vegetable aspic or actually consume it.

I wrote the art gallery immediately to find out if this was really going to happen, Karl Lagerfeld strutting his fish-soufflé-eating self into this exhibition. I was assured that, yes, Karl was in fact supposed to appear in the flesh to fete an exhibition of photographs of Brad Kroenig he took for a book that consisted entirely of photographs of Brad Kroenig. The Amazon.com description of *Metamorphoses of an American: A Cycle of Youth 2003–2008* reads:

> *In* Metamorphoses of an American, *Karl Lagerfeld documents the physical and emotional development of Brad Kroenig, the world's most sought-after male model . . . Lagerfeld discovered Kroenig in 2003, making his first photographs of the young man in Biarritz; since then, he has diligently observed Kroenig through the photographic lens, month by month.*

The weirdest part of this whole event was that Karl would spend five years photographing one male model in order to put his obsession on full display in an art gallery in, of all places, midtown. (There were likely also openings in other exotic cities like Venice and Seoul, but let's just focus on New York City.) Being in midtown feels like being in a never-ending line at Starbucks. Isn't that why publishing houses like Hearst maintain such glamorous in-office cafeterias? So that their beautiful employees don't have to subject themselves to the distress of midtown for any extended length of time?

Of course, the problem with the opening being in midtown was that Karl Lagerfeld now had a really good excuse not to show up. But I had faith that it was my destiny to meet Fashion's Santa in the flesh, and so to Karl I went.

I recruited two companions for Operation Stalk Karl Lagerfeld at Random Midtown Art Gallery: (1) My friend Chris, fashion enabler and endearingly speechless in the face of any meaningful celeb, most especially Madonna. Necessary for moral support in case I found myself speechless in Karl's presence. And (2) NYmag .com's videographer Jonah. Necessary to capture an interview for the website and the personal files I'd need if I ever felt like bragging about this occasion over the next several decades of my life.

We arrived that misty Friday night and rode the elevator up to the gallery, which had gray walls that were absolutely covered in photos of Brad Kroenig. There was Brad looking out a window, there was Brad looking at his sleeve, there was a collage of wallet-sized images of Brad's face. We were all willfully trapped in a chamber of Bradness. Fortunately, they were serving free wine.

"What are you going to say to Karl?" Chris asked, eyes wide.

"Omigosh." I was beginning to get tipsy and forget my plan, which amounted to engaging Karl in a brief but rousing discourse about sexism as it relates political candidates' sartorial choices. All

I could think of, though, was, "Do you only have acquired tastes, or do you like normal things, too?" and "Does Brad come with vocal cords? If so, does it matter?"

So, we waited. Chris and I decided Brad was attractive. Worthy of five years of documentation and an entire $80 art book attractive? Well, that at least gave us something to talk about. Seven o'clock turned to seven thirty, which turned to eight, which turned to . . . nine. Friends came, gave up on Karl, and left to go fist pump at nightclubs. One glass of wine turned to three. We forgot that it was weird that the face of one man surrounded us on all sides. I longed for the ordeal to end. Though I believed in Karl—have *always* believed in Karl—I started to wonder if he would materialize in this gray cell of his own imagination or if Brad would simply whisk him away to an Olsen twin's house for a nice cold meal of aspic.

"He's not coming," Chris said.

"Don't talk like that," Jonah countered. "He'll come. Keep the faith." Even though Jonah was not of the world of fashion, he somehow understood a few basic rules: that Karl is God, God is worth waiting for, and that God arrives on God's own schedule.

"Well if he *doesn't* show up, we can't feel too bad about getting stood up by Karl Lagerfeld," I pointed out. Just think of the countless rock-hard abs that went unseen by Karl for the entire five years that he only had eyes for Brad's. Besides, "It's not like we found him on JDate."

Just as I decided the invitation's promise—*Karl Lagerfeld will be present*—was a lie and resigned myself to heading home drunk with no story to show for it, the elevator doors parted, and out strode the man, the myth, the Karl. You know how you feel when you've been at a concert forever, waiting for the artist to come on, and your feet hurt, and you're blaming the person you paid too much to see and vowing to hate her forever, when all of a sudden the lights go down and smoke fills the stage, and suddenly Britney Spears or J. Lo emerges from an oversized floor tile, and everything is worth it? That's pretty much exactly how Karl entered the room. Except his version of backup dancers are middle-aged men in suits.

This was our moment. The camera light turned on and we moved toward Karl. Because this was fate, Karl moved right toward us, like we were all Brad Kroenig.

"*Karl!!!* Karl. Karl, why Brad?" I shoved the mic in his face.

"I thought he had the ease with the camera very, very few people have," Karl said. He leaned in close when he talked to me. He smelled like soap. "I thought, he can transform himself."

When interviewing God at a cocktail party, you have to remember that everyone around you is going to want a little piece of God. Whether it's a selfie with God, an acknowledgment from God, or a photo of God—he's going to be an in-demand member of the party. So, if you need a little piece of God—witty banter about an election, for instance—you'll have to get the obligatory small talk out of the way quickly before God is understandably distracted by a man with abs that look like a freshly baked challah loaf.

"Do you prefer Barack or Hillary?"

Karl reminded me—and what would probably be our five viewers—that he's foreign. "There's nothing worse than strangers having an opinion of something that does not concern them," he said.

"But what do you think of Hillary's pantsuits," I sputtered as he began to pull away. *Was Brad tugging on his ponytail? Fuck off, Brad!*

"Women in politics have a big problem," he said. "If they are too chic they don't look serious so it's very, very difficult. I think her pants are poorly cut."

And then he moved away to get his photo taken and gaze at the walls.

I remember feeling somewhat delirious after the interview. It was like seeing a really good concert from the front row where the artist leans over to high-five you. Also I wasn't drunk or high and there was no crowd that caused exiting the venue to make you feel like swearing off concerts till the end of time.

.   .   .

If I could have such a positive experience with Karl, I could surely have one with Rachel a couple years later, when I had more experience and knew I could get through celebrity encounters without being weird. But I was afraid of what she'd think of me after so many years of blogging about her reality show, her QVC line, and her husband's affinity for leather jewelry. For all I knew, she could have a voodoo doll that she stuck with an extra pin every time I wrote "Rachel's husband, who wears more necklaces at once than I own."

I arranged to meet Rachel at Saks, where she was doing a launch event for her clothing line. It was part party and part "Rachel tells people who spend a lot of money at Saks what to buy from her clothing line." I was excited but extremely nervous that I'd be berated for being a snarky bitch.

When I arrived at Saks, I rode the escalators to the corner of a floor manned by a secretary at a dark wood desk. That's how you know you're in a really fancy store—they have secretaries at desks to keep the riffraff out of the secret "backstage" areas that regular people aren't supposed to know exist. Going to a special area to interview a famous person like this is always a little nervous-making, because it heightens the differences between that person's life and your own. But it's also hardly unexpected. A famous stylist as recognizable as Zoe isn't going to stand next to the sale rack to talk to me when she could be in a nice enclosed room with comfortable furniture and silver trays of tea sandwiches.

The secretary ushered me through a door. Behind that door was another desk manned by another secretary. That secretary had a woman wearing all black guide me through a maze of heavy doors and secret passageways lined with plush carpeting. Very often when you are going to meet a celebrity you will have to navigate the intestines of a very large building. They like to hide in rooms deep within these places that no one aside from other famous people ever knew existed. My gallery encounter with Karl was so unusual because he usually pulls this very trickery—once I tried to interview him at Macy's and couldn't because I was told I was "not on the list," but in reality I had no idea if he was even physically *there*, since the only indication of his presence was a bunch of suits guarding a dark hallway.

Eventually my escort established me in a room with a lovely display of tiny sandwiches and refreshments. Those wildly popular ten-dollar bottles of green juice were chilling in a silver ice bucket. Because the new hotness at press junkets now is to treat overpriced green juice like fine champagne. To be fair, eight of them probably cost as much as a bottle of Dom. Everyone takes one, but no one drinks it because they like it—they just take it because they know it retails for ten dollars. It's the Birkin bag of beverages.

Then I waited. Interviewing designers and celebrities always involves waiting because there are always eight million other people who want something from them and fame is a constant act of figuring out who deserves to be fit in and when. I probably fit in somewhere below "have assistant replace old socks" on these people's to-do lists.

As I sat there with the ice bucket of overpriced juice waiting for Rachel, I thought about all the arguably negative things the Cut had posted about her. It all started with a freelancer reporting that Rachel missed Marc Jacobs's show (because he had the gall to start on time instead of thirty minutes late like everyone else) and was upset by it. As one would be if they missed Marc Jacobs's show for the reason that he started on time! Because this is a fact of every woman's life: *no one is on time*. The blog post was even splashed on the screen in the middle of an episode of her Bravo reality show. Which shall stand forever in my mind as the closest I've ever been to appearing on Bravo. But as joyous as I was about the Cut's airtime, it came at the cost of even more airtime of Rachel in her signature outfit—the white hotel bathrobe—looking quite upset over the whole thing. *Did she still hate me?* If she did, she might force me to explain why we published that she missed Marc Jacobs's show and ask why I was so mean and don't I know that she's a real person just like everyone else? *If she threw green juice on me, would it stain?* I was about to find out.

Carrie came into the room before Rachel. She was tiny and stylish and perfectly lovely in person. But there was an edge to her voice that said she could turn off her niceness as soon as she wanted. Before Rachel Zoe came into the room, we exchanged polite conversation about how amazing she is. This is a ritual that seems to happen prior to interviewing nearly any major celeb. Maybe celebrities send their publicists in first to make sure the reporter will say she thinks the celebrity is the best thing that ever happened to the world. This must be the LA equivalent of a burning sage air cleanse.

Then Rachel breezed into the room, as if carried by the skirt of her long, flowing printed blue dress that was basically a daytime gown. Despite this being August, she wore the frock's pussy bow knotted high around her neck and a glossy black leather jacket over a top. Not that she looked the least bit uncomfortable or out of place, especially next to her assistant, who was wearing a full black tuxedo pantsuit from the line and quite possibly might have had all the oil glands in her face removed. Rachel always wears what Rachel wants, not what's practical. This is the beauty of being famous, and this is especially the beauty of working in fashion: no one expects the things you do, and certainly not the things you wear, to make sense. In fact, people *prefer* that you make very little sense. Hence, we have pop stars who wear '80s workout leotards to go shopping in New York in December. Hence, we have Karl Lagerfeld making $2,400 purses out of hula hoops.

Rachel was *lovely*. Perfectly welcoming and didn't say anything about how the Cut previously hurt her feelings. I definitely wouldn't have taken as kindly to anyone who made me upset on Bravo.

"The line looks so expensive!" I told Rachel when we shook hands near the snacks that no one would eat. A rack of the clothes she created hung yonder from the festering food. These included: a camel cape, a coat with a faux fur hem so thick that it looked like it had a fur skirt sewn on, suiting with flared pants that skimmed the ground, ruffled dresses, sequined jackets, and fur vests.

"Would you like to sit down? Have a seat in my office," she joked, plopping down on the couch. I obliged.

"So what made you want to do the line?" I asked.

"It was something that I have thought of a million times, but also the thing that I was petrified to do. I think being judged by my peers is something that is very scary to me. I have sat with these buyers and fashion directors of these retail stores for many, many years. And the editor in chiefs and things—the thought of being judged by them is petrifying. Petrifying."

I knew what she meant. People with outsize personas like Karl Lagerfeld are scary because you've no way of knowing whether what they're really like matches public perception until you interact. And then there's Fashion Week, which could be called "Judge Shit Week." We judge the clothes on the runway; we judge the designers, like Rachel and Karl, who design them; we judge the models wearing them; we judge the clothes people in attendance are wearing; we judge where everyone's sitting and what everyone is doing. And the most discomfiting part about all of it is that nothing anyone thinks is out in the open. With the exception of a few fashion critics, no one's willing to come out and say what they say to their coworkers when they're back at their offices or out of earshot. But you get alone with these people and you hear *everything*: which designer they think is terrible and should go out of business, which street-style star they think is a walking joke, which front-row celebrity they think is the most desperate, which editor they think is the most lame.

As someone who's been on the inside of the business for two decades, Rachel knows this well. She also knows that hers is a business of image making where all that matters is the first impression. Fashion isn't like pop songs that you have to hear several times before you fall in love with them. People fall in love with clothes or outright hate them immediately. Very few fashion designers get the chance to woo people over time—the ones who do manage to churn out hit after hit season after season until they train their audiences to embrace everything they do as genius. When you are just starting out and are a known reality TV star—in the snooty eyes of the fashion industry, the polyester of fame—you have to work even harder to get people to see your cred.

I asked Rachel why she did a line that stores classify as "contemporary," which means expensive but not horrifically expensive. Most celebs do cheapo lines for stores like Sears and Walmart. But these Rachel Zoe dresses were $400 and would be sold at Saks, a floor away from $800 to $2,000 Alexander McQueen and Stella McCartney dresses. To Zoe, who is rich, the contemporary category is probably her Target.

"I was really maniacal about keeping prices down," Zoe said. "I am such a fan of Victoria Beckham and Marc Jacobs. All these designers are—I mean, are you kidding me?"

Here's something I love about Rachel Zoe: what you see is what you get. You have an idea of her in your head, and then you get there, and she's just like you imagined her but even more so. Even though she dresses up all the time and always has her hair and makeup done professionally, even though her publicist is completely scary, even though she's important enough to warrant silver platters of tea sandwiches every time she sits in a room, there's something down to earth about her. She's not like an actress who's seemingly *really really* nice to the *New Yorker* profile writer and then a total bitch to a party reporter on a red carpet. *(Claire Danes.)* You can connect with her, whereas someone like Karl Lagerfeld is so out there that you sometimes wonder if he's actually a piece of technology that winds up in the back. But what Karl and Rachel have in common is the ability to translate their personalities to iconic looks and then turn those iconic looks into mass-appeal design.

"I remember there were certain pieces that I loved the sample, I really loved the sample, and I would sit with my design team and it was like, this is this amount of money. And I was like, I'm not going above that price point. It's too expensive."

This is an admirable viewpoint for a designer who can and will spend more on one handbag than many people will spend on their college educations.

Rachel took me over to the rack of clothes to show me some of the pieces. "This is the Charlie suit, although I don't see the bottom here. This has shorts, long shorts, pants, all different pieces," she said. "It's very Saville Row." (Saville Row is a street in London where David Beckham buys custom-made suits that cost as much as designer wedding dresses.)

"Tuxedos," Rachel said, still flipping. "Look at Mandana. Stand up," Rachel ordered the thin, dark-haired young woman perched yonder on a couch. She rose and kicked her feet around a bit so that I got the full effect of her flared pants.

"Very flattering," I reassured her.

After some more riveting conversation about fabric samples and how to choose just the right sequins, Rachel had to be received by her people. I tagged along. Because a person of importance never walks a hallway alone, a group of several of us, including Rachel and her publicist and others who were apparently involved in this operation, were led down more secret passageways until we got to what I can only assume was a very elite fitting room.

Doors were open like some sort of advent calendar to reveal ladies dressed in Rachel's line, one after the other. Rachel's job was to go from room to room advising them on how to wear her stuff. This is *styling*.

Rachel educated one strawberry blond seventeen-year-old

shopping with her mom on where the seams of the sleeves on her sequin blazer should hit for the best slouch. "I like to wear it a little bigger so you can wear a zero or a two or a four," she said, flying in the face of every woman's logic that one should buy the smallest size possible at all times, which is why my father always said he wanted to open a clothing store and call it Size Two, where everything inside would be a size two, which is really all every woman wants. She also assured a hedge fund manager in the next room that the camel cape she was trying on was "insta-chic," should she have had any fears about looking like an Upper East Side superman in it.

You would think that these women—bankers, high schoolers with their moms—would freak out about getting styled by the world's most famous stylist (I had become comfortable talking to Rachel but would have been mortified for her to judge my clothes). But I guess because this is New York and nothing is less cool than freaking out over celebrities here, they acted as though having Rachel Zoe style them was as normal as ordering a skim extra foam latte at the local Starbucks. Shopping at Saks a lot had awarded them this tutelage, and they would not grovel in the face of it. Then again, E! and celebrity lifestyle websites tell every woman that she deserves to feel like Gwyneth Paltrow for at least a day out of every year—and if you have a Saks frequent-flyer card, that standard probably goes up to at least a day out of every month.

After our visit in Saks, I spoke to Rachel once again on the phone while she was getting chauffeured home from another store event. She was lovely again even though I felt like I was being a huge pest. This is the job of a reporter: to nag and stalk and nag until you get what you need. It's like dealing with the cable company: you can bother them as much as you want, but no matter how many fireworks you set off to get them to look twice at you, you're still at the mercy of their automated answering system.

I ended up writing a story that was quite positive about Rachel and her clothing line. Ultimately, I had no evidence to support any of the weirdo internet rumors about her injecting celebrities and faux fur vests with horse drugs. Also, no one said she was a hack and that her line was a hack job and that the faux fur felt like a broom. Everyone loved her and her line and thought she was brilliant. I did not forget the call I received from Carrie in the beginning that served as a warning against me doing a snarky hack job on Rachel. But after you hang out with someone and she's nice to you, it's quite hard to write something mean about her anyway. Things would have been different, of course, if she *had* thrown Saks Fifth Avenue's tuna salad at my hair.

After the story went up and Fashion Week was about to start, I received warning that a "tree" had manifested itself on my desk.

Given that I've killed a cactus, this was as concerning as it was exciting.

When I got to work, I saw that it was an orchid about half my height. Somewhere within the reams of cellophane and massive white flowers dangling off the thing, there was a card.

"Thanks for your kind words!—Rachel" it read.

I still have the card. Rachel is likely to be the most influential stylist/celebrity/designer to exist in my lifetime, so having a note from her is major. The orchid is long gone unfortunately, but the card is something I can show my kids one day when Rachel is the new Karl Lagerfeld, trotting around the globe in a powdered wig plugging erotic coffee-table ebooks about her husband's chest hair. By the time they're old enough to read, handwriting will be as out of style as cave paintings.

• 4 •

Celebrities

GOING BRA-LESS INTO THE CELEBRITY WILD

H ow is that?" Richard Gere asked, gesturing to my scallops.

"Not amazing," I replied, wondering immediately if I should have lied.

"Try one of these," he said, sliding one of his ravioli onto my bread plate. Either he was generous, really thought the ravioli was that good, just fucking with me because he could see how nervous I was, or on a low-carb diet. (Hollywood people.)

I cut it in half and took a bite.

"I like it," he assured me. It tasted like pumpkin pie.

"Me too," I said. (*This* was the time to lie.)

Seated to my other side at the round table was a film journalist who was really excited to get to talk about Bob Dylan, the subject of the movie Richard Gere was eating ravioli to promote. I am about as capable of discussing Bob Dylan with enthusiasm and expertise as I am Jell-O, scientifically proven to be some of the most repulsive edible material on earth. I was covering the dinner as a party reporter and freelancer for *New York* mag—one of the many such assignments I took hoping it would turn into full-time work—and the youngest and unquestionably most uncomfortable person at this table (also, the sole woman). I felt too nervous and out of my comfort zone to engage in conversation. I felt like I was eating dinner with a bunch of other people's dads. Dads who like to talk about football and listen to classic rock and eat wings. Whereas I'm much more of a watch *Sex and the City*, listen to Britney Spears, eat hummus and baby carrots sort of person. I felt enough out of my element at fashion events, which I covered more than any other kind, so being faced with Richard Gere's ravioli was especially scary.

I was reporting on a dinner and screening for a movie Gere appeared in about Bob Dylan called *I'm Not There*. The more of these events I could cover, well, the more likely I was to be seen as a strong candidate for a job like the one I landed later at the Cut. When my editor told me to go to the dinner preceding the screening I had no idea that I would be seated right next to Richard Gere and the director of the film, Todd Haynes. Here's the thing: I actually don't get that into movies most of the time unless they're ninety minutes or less, a rom-com (again, ninety minutes or less), or involve space exploration in a non-sci-fi fashion. Talking about movies and '60s music comes about as naturally to me as watching any sport that doesn't involve a leotard. When I see a football game on TV, my brain registers nothing beyond the glass of the television set, and I involuntarily enter a state of extreme boredom.

Am I supposed to interview these people? I wondered. *Isn't it weird to interview people who are maybe extending the hand of friendship by giving you their ravioli? Yes, it's totally weird. Act natural. Eat the ravioli.*

As I chewed, I noticed the conversation had turned to something I actually had things to say about: iPods! At the time, these were a new invention.

"Do you have an iPod?" I asked Gere.

Yes, he said, but only for research purposes. "I don't like those things in my ears," he said. "I don't like headphones, I think music sounds better without headphones." He would later pull a flip phone out of his pocket. Such a dad move to be four cell phone models behind everyone else.

Maybe I can just switch the recorder on and set it on the table.

I knew I had to come back with something. My editor would wonder how I could eat an entire meal with Richard Gere and not come back with anything but a story about how Gere gave me some of his pasta.

I switched on my recorder and set it next to the plate where Gere's ravioli gift formerly lay.

As a party reporter, I was used to interviewing celebrities in the safety of a cocktail party, where you could scoot away to a bar and cajole with other party reporters as soon as you finished asking your awkward questions. I was not used to having entire meals with celebrities and geeky film buffs who actually want to have serious conversations about someone's art or craft. In my mind, people want to know things about celebrities that make them human—like if they wear underwear with holes or floss regularly.

After the meal ended, with me functioning at no higher a human level than the centerpiece, I panicked.

I just lost a whole hour that I could have been interviewing Richard Gere about something hilarious, like his favorite celebrity cat or if he'd ever given up dairy products and did that make him feel like kind of a woman?

Fuckity fuck fuck!

There would be an opportunity to get some quotes on the red carpet before the screening began. I ran to it and took my spot behind the rope that separates the famous from those who make them so. The divide between Them and Me bolstered my confidence a little bit.

"I just wanted to ask you some questions I didn't think of during dinner!" I spewed at Todd Haynes when he came by.

"Did you ever talk to Dylan?" I asked.

"I didn't talk to Dylan at all. I could've, but I chose not to," he said. "I didn't really need the real guy sitting there and me asking the kind of questions that people ask him, and kind of putting him back in that box like, 'Is it true that you said this or are you really into rock 'n' roll and not folk anymore?' You know what I mean?" (No.) "The film plays so much with the mask, the myth making rather than the real thing that he might say on that day at that moment. And I didn't want to put him in that position, you know?" (No.)

Shit. Have nothing Really Real to say about Dylan. Change conversation topic. I know: animals.

"Richard said at dinner you never asked him if he rode a horse. You never did?"

"I didn't tell Richard—well, it was in the script, but I never asked him, 'Do you know how to ride a horse really good?' And then it was like a week into it, and he was riding the horse everywhere and he turned to me and he was like, 'Pretty good I ride a horse, huh?'"

"HAHAHA thanksomuchforyourtime!" I said, scared-like. And then he moved down the line to the next person.

After I sat through the film, I dashed home to review my recordings. The dinner conversation was completely inaudible.

I filed something about my experience sitting next to Richard

Gere at dinner, like a total creeper. Fortunately, my editors liked it enough to run it online.

Considering I had covered maybe a couple dozen or so parties for *New York* magazine up to that point, I really had ample experience speaking coherently to famous people not to botch that assignment. The great thing about party reporting, if you're shy like me, is that it extinguishes the natural human instinct to avoid extremely embarrassing and awkward situations. I am a quiet, introverted person, and when I first started, I would feel terrified with nerves. Shy introverts will understand when I say that nothing feels worse than being at a cocktail party alone, especially trying to talk to strangers at a cocktail party you've attended alone. I had to resist every impulse to run out the door or do things on my cell phone to look like I wasn't a terrified, introverted loser. I'm about as type A as they come, so succeeding at the assignments was good enough motivation for me to suck it up and go through with every terrifying encounter. The job is simple: you go up to famous people at swanky parties, introduce yourself, and ask them all kinds of questions you wouldn't ask unless you were conducting an interview. When I started, I was terrified of talking to these people. But I built up a tolerance to the awkwardness, and it eventually became relatively not-scary.

On any given night in New York, at least half a dozen celebrity red-carpet events take place. Many of these are fashion events, because fashion people love to have parties for everything, especially store openings and perfume launches. Each fashion show that has celebrities at it is covered as its own little one-hour party. Once my editor learned how much I loved *Project Runway*, she sent me mostly to fashion events and shows when Fashion Week rolled around. But designers, models, and other fashion people often show up to other stuff happening around town, like film premieres, so fashion knowledge always came in handy.

Interviews can be about as comfortable as rectal exams, which is to say: neither party really *wants* to go through with it, but since the livelihood of each is at stake, the discomfort becomes a necessary evil. Overall, parties are seldom the place for serious discussions—people are drinking, it's noisy, and you usually have only three or so minutes to get a famous person to say something worth printing before their hovering publicist lightly taps you on the back, which is party speak for, "Thanks, dear, please fuck off now." For *New York* magazine, standard sound bites like "I love pink lip gloss! I wear it every day" weren't printable. You had to come back with something much funnier or weirder or newsier.

At parties, it's best to open the interview by asking something relating to the event at hand. For instance, if you're at Roberto Cavalli's Halloween party, you would ask questions about Halloween, the merits of wearing leopard versus giraffe print, and things that happen on yachts, because all these things relate to Cavalli and the odious day you're "celebrating." (Yes, I have Halloween Hate, which is a natural reaction to October 31 when three years in a row the night has ended with you drunk-crying on your floor, and you live in one of three cities in the country where grown adults get more excited over wearing costumes than four-year-olds who go trick or treating do.)

After I was assigned to a party, my editors would give me some suggested questions to ask the celebrity guests. For example, for P. Diddy's launch party for his Sean John fragrance Unforgivable

Woman, my editor suggested I ask people, "What do you smell like?"

"It's a good question for a fragrance party," she said. "I always ask that." Dutifully, I went for it.

This Unforgivable Woman launch party was held in a town house on the Upper East Side with hardly any lights on inside. At this Chateau de Diddy, the air was filled with the unfortunate stench of both the Unforgivable Woman fragrance and a fog machine that, judging by the putrid nature of its excretions, had to have been a health hazard.

I figured that my best chance for interviewing celebs at this thing was staking out the staircase leading to a purportedly glamorous attic-type enclosure where Diddy had sequestered himself with fellow celebrities like Ashton Kutcher and some other Chosen Hot Women. Collectively, these people are known Manhattan-wide as VIPs, which loosely translates to "Various Inflated Personalities." These VIPs moved toward this fateful staircase, past a velvet rope guarded by linebackers wearing elegant black suits. I caught Jay Z about to ascend the stairs to Diddy's lair with Beyoncé. As he walked by and got rushed by reporters just like me, I thrust my tape recorder in front of his chest and shouted, "WHAT DO YOU SMELL LIKE????" The absurdity of the question and, surely, the aggression and desperation with which I asked it, prompted him to pause before me and deliver a truly spectacular answer.

"Oh, I smell incredibly beautiful," he said, waving his arms about with passion. "I smell like you just got out of the shower, you have on the towel, and you just got your sheets on your bed, and you're laying, and you wrap yourself up. I smell like that."

I'd smell like that, too, if I hadn't spent an hour sweating in Casa de Unforgivable.

Later, when Jay and Bey finished their partying in Diddy's private lair and descended the stairs, I managed to catch Beyoncé herself, dressed in a black satin dress that was very "high school semiformal." (Maybe it was from Diddy's Sean John clothing line.) I asked her the same question. She only said she felt "hot"—before fleeing the premises. So I guess Diddy's VIP suite didn't feature the one thing everyone in the building longed for more than a paper bag to breathe into, which was air conditioning.

I spent two hours desperately seeking celebrities and perspiring at the bottom of those stairs. A reporter whom I had befriended over the course of this tedious display of Diddy's Unforgivable Ego spotted film mogul Harvey Weinstein in the darkness, within the haze of Unforgivable perfume and even more Unforgivable steam.

"My editor wouldn't be interested in him. But you can definitely talk to him—he's so *New York* mag," she said. I had no idea who Harvey Weinstein was at the time (this was long before I turned myself into street-style bait and bumped into him at the Plaza), but I was growing desperate for some material I could file. So I parted the sea of models that surrounded him, approached, and asked him the same question Jay Z had liked so much. I would prove myself fearless in the face of such awkwardness yet again. What could possibly go wrong?

"What do you smell like?" I said, adding that signature fake giggle that says, "I like talking to you!" This helps a party reporter seem at least slightly personable. As Weinstein's expression darkened, I realized that I had made a bad decision. Very bad. And I was about to get yelled at for my Unforgivable question.

"What do I smell like?" he growled. "What do you *mean*, 'What do I smell like?'" He then instructed me to turn off my recorder and growled more nasty things to my face, which I've since blacked out from my memory. When the verbal abuse ended, I returned to my post beside the banister, a little embarrassed but not really because Jay Z and I had just had a positively *brilliant* one-question interview. To become good at this kind of work, you must be impervious to willful interactions with people that end up feeling like self-flagellation. Over the course of my yearlong party reporting career, I loosened up and stopped freaking out about approaching or talking to celebrities and eventually became, if not comfortable, than at least not nervous when talking to fashion people like Marc Jacobs and Tim Gunn. When I started, I refused to drink at the events because I felt I had to concentrate. Several months in, I drank freely and began to treat celebrities like extremely cute pets out for a walk. When it was my turn for some face-to-face time, I coddled them briefly before moving on to the real questions I wanted to ask. At the end of the night, what really mattered was how Jay Z stopped to tell me he smelled like bath soap. All the celebrities who refused to answer my questions became great stories I told at cocktail parties when people found out what I did for a living and wanted to know who's actually an asshole.

I should say most celebs you interview at parties are a *lot* nicer than Weinstein. I believe he was the meanest to me of all the people I've ever tried to interview. Most of the time when people don't want to talk to reporters, they're nice about it. For instance: once I went up to Kanye West after a Rodarte fashion show and innocently queried, "A couple questions?"

"No questions," he replied. I must have looked exceedingly sad at his answer, because he then said, "A*www*," and gave me a side hug—you know the kind—where he didn't want to fully, intimately hug me front-to-front so he put his arm around me from the side and gave me a comforting squeeze. I can still feel Kanye's scruff against my cheek from that, the most defining side hug of my career. I also distinctly remember him smelling nice, which meant he was definitely *not* wearing Unforgivable Woman.

Some celebrities are really mean to reporters at parties and have a reputation among party reporters for being nasty. When I was on the circuit, Kirsten Dunst was really curt with a friend of mine who interviewed her at a party, and Claire Danes acted awfully unhappy with me when I tried to interview her at the premiere of a boring movie I bet she would never want to talk about now that you probably don't even remember existing called *Evening*. (The most significant thing about *Evening* is that she met her husband, Hugh Dancy, while filming it.) My editor told me stories about Rachel Weisz; other reporters on the scene had stories about how Julianne Moore wouldn't give them the time of day even if they had a million-dollar check in her name taped to their foreheads.

. . .

But truly, most celebs are nice if you approach them properly. And then there are the people who are *exceedingly* nice. Like Sarah Jessica Parker, with whom I once enjoyed a groundbreaking eight-minute encounter at a Ralph Lauren fashion show.

This fashion show was nicer than most people's weddings, and practically every guest was a celebrity or socialite. Celebrities are vital to many labels. They help draw reporters to a designer's events, increasing exposure for the label, and, because they're usually dressed by the designer before showing up, serve as templates for that designer's version of glamour. The night began with me learning the event was black tie. Normally, to reporters, black tie just means "no jeans" unless you're a female or male television red carpet personality, in which case you show up to everything wearing full sparkles and spray foundation. I don't own any ball gowns and had low expectations of the fanciness of the event—often dressing in true "black tie" seems unnecessary because many people just show up wearing cocktail dresses and suits anyway. I just needed to find my least offensive dress, one that would not make people who wear designer clothes daily feel repelled by my presence. I was between a printed wool Banana Republic shift dress and a black jersey halter dress I dug out of a bin at the Calypso St. Barth sample sale. The black Calypso dress was obviously a better option, as it did not make me resemble a 1960s area rug. However: this dress did not allow for a bra. And was I mentally prepared to go braless into the celebrity wild? This was a huge ask of my psyche considering how easily I embarrass.

I tried on the dress, which had a wide piece of fabric that wrapped around my chest and tied in the back, leaving slivers of skin exposed around my outer upper rib cage and back. I had to pull it as tightly as possible in the back to minimize the risk of nipping.

Is this see-through?

It didn't look see-through in the makeup mirror in my bedroom. I am small-chested and my boobs looked like sideways hard-boiled eggs underneath my dress, but that was probably less embarrassing than showing up in something arguably hideous. This was clearly my most elegant wardrobe option, and my boobs would have to brave being one layer of jersey fabric away from whichever famous people we had to speak to. If all else failed, I could always cross my arms.

As soon as I arrived at the show in Central Park, I realized this was the opposite of a hippie-dippie leave-your-bra-at-home rendezvous. No one would collapse in a fog of hallucinogens inside a tee-pee here, most definitely not. Rather, this was the kind of place you went only if (1) you actually owned formal evening wear, (2) employed a stylist to tape your bust into your bra-prohibitive dresses, or (3) designed much of the evening wear in attendance yourself.

Fuck.

Prior to red carpet events, publicists send reporters a "tip sheet" that tells you which celebrities are expected to attend. You have to view tip sheets like horoscopes—they may be right; they may be pure fantasy. This event was not the latter—it had so many celebrities, the staircase they entered from was a veritable celebrity waterfall. Diane Sawyer, Barbara Walters, Vera Wang, Donna Karan, Martha Stewart, Mayor Bloomberg—one after the other, they pummeled me with their fame and accompanying scariness. At least they couldn't be scarier than Harvey Weinstein post–"What do you smell like?"

I was nervous, less so about the high concentration of famous people than the reality that if I failed to come back with an assload of printable material, my editor would never give me another assignment ever again. But I imagined physically setting my fear aside in a bush and rapidly intercepted one after the other, lobbing them question after ridiculous question.

"Barbara Walters! How do you survive Fashion Week?"

She looked at me with wide eyes. "You're very pretty, but I cannot answer your questions."

On to Diane Sawyer: "Diane! Can you share a good story about Ralph?"

She recalled going to interview him for the first time. "All of a sudden, I'm thinking, *Why did I wear these shoes? How could I inflict this outfit on him?*"

YES! Vera Wang, please bestow your wit upon my tape recorder now?

"He asked me what I thought about a jacket [during a job interview] and I said, 'Well I don't know if I really like it,' and then he hired me."

Martha Stewart talked about Ralph's loud and expensive cars. I was flourishing like the most popular girl at the party who came alone and made everyone fall in love with her. I was the opposite of a centerpiece. I was like Carrie Bradshaw at a sorority mixer.

After the arrivals, the black-tie Mega Event officially began with a runway show with the kind of stadium-style bench seating that allows you to see the full torso of everyone in attendance. This gives everyone who's not seated in the front row a fair chance at seeing the clothes. It also—and this is just as important at a fashion show—lets everyone judge their compatriots' outfits across the aisle and makes everyone feel like everyone else is staring at them, which fashion people obviously want all the time. Because I wasn't wearing a bra and, therefore, felt that much more nervous about being in this place, I was extremely attuned to the possibility of famous people staring at me. *What if my boobs are showing through the dress under the bright lights?*

Once the *My Fair Lady*–themed show ended, Ralph Lauren took his rightful spot at the end of the runway, flourished his hand like the Wizard of Oz, and the runway backdrop painted with a scene of horses at the races magically parted behind him to reveal a garden party low-lit with candles. A fountain spurted. Champagne awaited. I felt like I was entering the enchanted land of *FernGully* only instead of fairies dotting the landscape there were *celebrities*. Hooray! You just had the feeling that Halle Berry or Renee Zellweger was somewhere within the twinkling darkness, perched atop a fantastical glittering mushroom. Everyone sighed in pleasure, utterly enthused by the fanciness Ralph was revealing to them, and applauded wildly, for here was a level of spendiness that perhaps even this crowd had not seen within the past two weeks.

I pushed forth into the great beyond, past Diane Sawyer, past Barbara Walters, past all the people who spent my monthly rent on a single pair of shoes, determined to reach Ralph before all of them.

"Ralph! Amazing show. How do you choose your opening models?" I began.

No special openers, he said. His shows include only "the most beautiful models in the world."

Great! "Are you going to other shows this Fashion Week?"

"No. No one invited me."

Hilarious! By then, the space surrounding Ralph had filled with so many of his devoted luminaries that I had been out-star-powered and the interview was up. This is what's magical about being a fashion designer: the world's most fabulous people are constantly groveling about you. Because who would they be without your fabulous clothes to wear? Fashion designers play a crucial role in celebrities' success, considering they're minimum 75 percent defined by how they look and whether or not that look conveys the certain *je ne sais quoi* required to keep people looking at you. (The other 24 percent comes from their talent, and the other 1 percent comes from people like me. Because all you have to do to be famous these days is show up and get photographed wearing outfits. If you feel like you want to be quoted somewhere, you write a caption for a selfie and post it to social media.)

One extreme upside to the elegant party lighting was that no one would be able to decipher my lousy braless look.

Once the crowd dispersed into the conservatory, I set about interviewing the rest of the celebrities positioned around the central fountain—spurting so hard it was splashing guests with nearly the same frequency as the plants. It was like a wax museum.

And right by the fountain was she, the deity worshiped by every New York twentysomething woman: ~~Carrie Bradshaw~~ Sarah Jessica Parker.

She looked every bit Carrie Bradshaw in a strapless glittering gown with an ankle-length tulle skirt. She wore a thick brown men's belt around her waist and had her hair pulled back tightly into one of those buns that rivals all baked goods. This was my chance not only to get a great quote, but, most importantly, *make best friends with Carrie Bradshaw.*

I double-checked my dress before gliding over to the fountain. She was alone save her husband Matthew Broderick, who is short and therefore easy for me to talk over.

"Sarah Jessica! Hi! I'm from *New York* magazine and—"

"Oh, I *love New York* magazine!" she said as though she wanted to just leave with me immediately and go dancing at the gay nightclub Splash.

I did foresee one immediate downside to being best friends with Carrie Bradshaw, which is that I couldn't *be* Carrie in our friend group. Sadly, I would have to be Miranda, because I didn't sleep around enough to be Samantha, and I definitely wasn't nearly as into the color pink as Charlotte. Miranda is obviously the one no one in a girls' friend group wants to be because she's so bitter and probably shops at Eileen Fisher, but I decided I could resign myself to such a fate if Carrie Bradshaw were the person I called when I didn't want to go to Pinkberry alone.

Carrie began telling me how much she loved *New York*'s restaurant reviews. I basically acted as if I wrote these myself, even though I had as little to do with those as I did making the *Sex and the City* movie, which she was currently working sixteen-hour days producing. (Shooting would start in ten days.) (I hoped this would leave us enough time to visit all the new cupcake stores.)

She revealed that she loved a recent feature on food carts in particular. "I'll eat anything if it's off a cart," she said, explaining that her favorite was this one on Sixth Avenue between Forty-Seventh and Fifty-Fifth.

"Um, do you worry about hygiene?" I asked.

"I think they're actually pretty vigilant about it," she answered. "They've got these businessmen standing in line for three hours to get their lunch . . . and you don't hear a lot of reports about intestinal issues."

"And how about dining options *not* on wheels?" *Will we get to eat at any of those together because I'm not really into food trucks, sister?*

"I don't know how to pronounce it correctly. S-f-o —" she began, referring to Sfoglia, a fancy Italian restaurant on the Upper East Side.

Then the conversation turned to Fashion Week. She was too busy to go to anything but this Ralph Lauren show. Besides, "There's so much scrutiny now," she said, referring to how the media picks apart everything about every celebrity. "People are so cruel, so I go to as few things as possible."

After eight minutes of thrilling conversation, another surefire *SATC* fanatic pulled my new best friend away from me, which created that awkward situation where I was forced to converse solo with her significant other, Matthew Broderick. Again, stuck with a dad.

"Can I ask you a few questions?" I asked. If his wife was so gleeful about talking to me, he should be, too. But, alas, he let out his sass.

"What did you think of the show?" I asked as a soft opener.

"I don't know anything about this stuff," he said, like he was *so over* the situation. Like he had been *dragged* there to this *girly* event and, oh God, *why* wasn't there a TV playing football, and would it have been *so much to ask* for the tuna tartar spoons to be sliders? You would think a theater actor would be right at home at a fashion show that resembled, well, theater, but no.

"What was the last show you went to?" I asked. If you're dating the world's premiere fashion icon, you have to have been to some of the best fashion events of all time.

Sure enough, he had been.

"I went to the big Valentino show in Rome."

"Oh! His retirement extravaganza." (You can watch footage of legendary designer Valentino Garavani's final show in the biopic about him, in which waiters wearing white gloves serve guests everything from foie gras terrine to, like, Triscuits.) "And how did that compare to this?"

"That was by the Coliseum," he said. "This is in Central Park."

I thanked him for his sassiness and then left to see people I have physical rather than imaginary friendships with at a normal bar.

Nothing ups your party game like an exchange with a celebrity. No conversation with a friend could be anywhere near as awkward. The downside is you naturally fall into interview mode and start talking to everyone as though everything about them could be a story. Fortunately, most of these people are flattered to know you think they're fabulous and actually care about where they bought their outfits.

· 5 ·

Editors

THE TIME I REFRAINED FROM BARFING ON MY IDOL,
ANNA WINTOUR

One hot summer afternoon the year following sweatpantsgate, I had prostrated myself on my sundeck for my annual two-month project of trying to turn my skin from translucent to a darker-than-white shade of opaque. Fortunately, I had not smoked any pot when my cell phone rang. "It's Mark Holgate," said a British-accented voice on the other end of the line belonging to a top-level editor at *Vogue* who had recently been promoted. "Would you be interested in interviewing for a fashion writer position at *Vogue?*"

Why, I—are cupcakes overrated? Are pandas the best kind of bear?

"*Yes*," I said into the phone. "Twist my arm."

"Great," Holgate said. "Can you send me your résumé and five clips? And contact HR so we can find a time for you to come in and meet Anna."

"Absolutely," I replied. "My life shall go on hold until these tasks are complete."

Vogue is seen as the bible of fashion magazines. Anna Wintour, its editor in chief, is therefore like the Creator of fashion. She is unquestionably the most influential and powerful person in the fashion industry. Working at *Vogue* meant you were, therefore, *also* one of the most influential and important people in the industry. It was a validation of one's own self-importance, and validating one's self-importance is, in many respects, the reason fashion exists in the first place.

Working at *Vogue* meant living a glamorous life not unlike that represented in *The Devil Wears Prada,* where you fly business class to Paris for Fashion Week, constantly attend private dinners with celebrities and famous designers, and get so many free and dis-counted designer clothes and spa treatments and gym memberships that you may as well be a B-list celebrity. The life of *Vogue*, it seems, is a never-ending whirlwind of wearing Manolo Blahnik pumps, elegant tablescapes, being thin, and being envied by everyone else in the industry. Naturally, rather than admit that *I* was jealous of the people who worked at *Vogue*, I would pretend like I was deeply turned off by their backward, stuffy ways. Since everyone is jealous of *Vogue* people but doesn't want to admit it, you can often find people to pretend they agree with you.

Naturally, as soon as they *call* you and dangle the opportunity in front of your face, you cease the shit talking and revert, teenager-like, to *Vogue* idol worship.

I realized I was sweating hard. (Did *Vogue* people sweat? Prob-ably not. Note to self: remove sweat glands before Anna inter-view.) It would only be a matter of time before the dye from my $25 neon Forever 21 bikini started bleeding into my precious white House of Deréon beach towel. Every time summer rolls around, this gift reaffirms my lying-out style as the embodiment of timelessness and elegance. I peeled myself off my towel and headed down to my apartment.

In my rapid descent to my Ikea-furnished studio, I did not stop to consider the true implications of working at *Vogue*. One, I'd have to go to work every day looking like I stepped out of the magazine in head-to-toe designer clothes and with professionally-done-looking hair and makeup, and here I already found it exhausting to get to my office in the most base-level nonpajama outfit—jeans, a Beyoncé T-shirt, flats—with my hair in a damp bun. Two, I'd have to write sunshine and daisies about everything in fashion, a far cry from my dryly humorous approach to writing about the business on the Cut. And three, I'd have to interview with Anna Wintour— my idol—with no barf bag at the ready.

Wait, I said to myself as the magnitude of this interview process began to sink in. *If I have to interview with Anna Wintour, how will I speak actual words to her face? And what on god's / her great earth am I going to wear?*

If only Tina Knowles had thrown in a skirt suit.

.   .   .

But of all the celebrity folk I intrepidly—and at times, igno-rantly—attempted to interview on New York's endless circuit of events promoting things that no one really cares about (like celeb-rity perfume), Anna Wintour was one I never had the balls to ap-proach. Anna, to me, is a great icon. The *greatest* icon. Few women command the same amount of respect, power, and influence as Anna. Whenever I have to do something scary and feel like I need an added cloak of confidence, I just imagine I'm Anna Wintour and act as though she would. For instance, say you're asking your boss for a raise. For many women—myself included—this is a scary thing to do. But wearing my invisible Anna costume, I can easily imagine myself walking into his office, sitting down in the chair opposite his desk, leaning back as though I have this conversation and wear $3,000 skirt suits every day, and saying, "You'll find my presence here has greatly improved the overall quality and class of this organization. For my services, I think you'll find an augmentation of my salary by thirty percent not only fair but also quite necessary. You simply just don't find talent like mine walking down Fifth Avenue any day of the week. I expect this adjustment to my pay to take effect immediately." And then I'd breeze out to Cipriani for lunch. Usually I can apply bits of this imagined reality to my life, and the resulting scene amounts to me tripping on the way into the office, developing hand tremors once I sit down, and barely making eye contact as I mumble how great I am and politely request more money. But this beats the alternative, which is not having the guts to ask for the raise at all.

So then, here's an awkward situation: how do you pretend to be the person who's interviewing you? I had no idea how I'd survive a face-to-face meeting with a woman I've looked up to my entire young adult and adult life. So, like the dutiful reporter I was, I started researching. I asked everyone I could think of in the media industry what interviewing with Anna was like. The most useful notes came in an email from an ex-*Vogue* employee who was friends with a friend. It read that I was "very far along" in the interview process if Anna Wintour herself was giving me time. My tipster also gave me four key tips. First, don't wear black because Anna is "all about color" (indeed, in a video posted to Vogue.com, she said the one thing she would never wear, unlike many a fashion person actually, is "head-to-toe black"). She also advised me to "have a life" because Anna will "ask more nonprofessional qs than professional," like what I do on the weekends. I was cautioned against claiming to be a tennis fan because Anna knows everything about it and there would be no way for me to fake it with her, which was no problem because even as much as I wanted to work at *Vogue* at that time, I'd never be able to convince anyone I was interested even remotely in any sort of sport that involves balls. Finally, she told me to mention an image or story from the magazine that I loved, and, perhaps most importantly, she cautioned me not to be thrown by Anna, who "is shy and of few words more than she's mean or anything like that. She won't bother to warm the room, usual throwaway niceties. It's just her way."

All I really had to do was study *Vogue*, wear not-black, not expect niceties, and speak intelligently about my hobbies. *Do I have hobbies?* I reasoned it was probably best not to go in there and say, "Matter of fact, I spend my weekends drinking and dancing to house music at nightclubs. Thanks to those brunch parties, you don't even have to go home anymore!" *Note to self: get hobbies.*

Despite my singular fear of Anna, and the possibility I didn't have any hobbies, I took some comfort in knowing that I had been edited by many high-profile magazine editors over the course of my career and had interviewed many more. But certain differences exist between editors who focus on text and editors who focus on visuals. You sort of have to look at it (and this is generalizing— many editors aren't exactly one type or the other) as the book nerds and the popular pretty kids in high school. Many editors who focus on textual storytelling won't look twice at what you wear so long as you show up wearing clothes. A fashion editor is likely to notice everything about your appearance. When I began working in fashion, I started noticing everything everyone around me wore. It was horrible—suddenly "that girl on the corner" becomes "that girl with the questionable gladiator sandals on the corner." Anna's background is as a fashion editor—a person who conceptualizes and styles fashion photo shoots. So I knew my outfit was absolutely key, as I have seen just how picky these editors can be. And indeed, it's an editor's job to be picky: editing is all about cutting stuff and redoing things until you end up with something perfect. Editors are constantly looking at things and trying to make them better. They are the gatekeepers between the runways and the general public, and ultimately after a runway show, the image of the clothes is in the hands of editors who choose (and are allowed) to photograph it.

My first expansive view into this world came when I had been working at the Cut for about two years and got assigned a story on Anna Dello Russo, the fashion director of Japanese *Vogue*. I interviewed her over the phone for *New York*'s spring fashion issue, and she described how she spent fifteen years working her way up from being an assistant who packs clothes for far-flung photo shoots to the spectacular fashion editor she is now. She studied fashion in university under Gianfranco Ferré and spent years toiling as an anonymous assistant and stylist before becoming internet-famous thanks to street-style photographers and her immaculate clothing collection. I admired her hard work and devotion to her job and the shameless glee with which she embraced the fame that didn't find her until middle age. Flaunting oneself becomes somehow not-obnoxious when the person doing the flaunting admits that's exactly what they're doing.

ADR is a woman who *truly* love love LOVES fashion. It's her breakfast, lunch, and dinner—in order to help accommodate her clothing collection, she has in fact edited the kitchen out of her home. She also keeps a separate apartment next to the gold-trimmed one she inhabits in Milan just for her clothes. She called this apartment her "studio" in our interview and explained that she even keeps it at a certain temperature so that she doesn't ruin her clothes.

"Collecting clothes is complicated because the clothes need a space and the right temperature, otherwise they get—you [can] really destroy clothes," she explained in her syrupy Italian accent. "It's dusty, it's hot—it ruins the clothes. I know very well how to store clothes, then everything is perfect. It's so freezing in my house! The clothes need to be cold."

I have a hard time imagining needing to store clothing in a temperature-controlled environment. But this is the difference between a woman who has "thousands" of pairs of designer shoes and a woman whose most prized items of apparel include a Beyoncé T-shirt and who interprets seaside elegance as a House of Deréon beach towel. For ADR, fashion is an attainable aspiration. For me, it's merely an aspiration. My chief clothing storage-related concerns amount to storing and packing my $25 bikinis so that they don't bleed neon dye into my Old Navy tank tops. As ADR described the ideal temperature for storing clothes, I found myself thinking of the layout of a grocery store: you have the warm part in the middle where the cheap, boring stuff like flour is, and the absolutely freezing part off to the side where they have the pricier, more exciting items like fish and meat and fine cheese. Having not been to ADR's apartment(s), I imagine the temperature scheme to be something like that. (Grocery stores, I get. High fashion, I'm still working on. Can you guess how that *Vogue* interview turned out?)

ADR became famous when street style started blowing up on the internet. She wore full runway looks to Fashion Week, and she wasn't borrowing these clothes—she was buying them herself. *With her own money.* (She won't say how much she spends on clothes.) A lot of people going to Fashion Week now borrow clothes, the way a celebrity does before going to the Oscars, so this might have been seen as even more eccentric behavior than the fact that she wears only the world's awesomest clothes and does not dress according to the season. What's more, once she's photographed in something, she goes home and changes, so she needs multiple outfits each day she goes to shows. I asked her about the process of packing for New York Fashion Week.

"Oh! Nightmare. I know very well packing—because that was my first job when I used to be fashion editor and travel around the world. We used to carry lot of stuff," she said. "If you arrive in Mexico, for example, and are shooting in chiffon, if you pack very well you will not iron clothes for three days. I had the best packing. I always teach my assistant how to pack the stuff the perfect way.

"Clothes for me are a religion," she continued. "I know how to pack, how to make it look good. So many times I see people . . . pack in a horrible way, and they need more volume, their dress is flat or something. One time I'll show you."

Oh, *will you now?* I was dying to take her up on her offer. Anything to interact with ADR in person and play with clothes.

At my next ideas meeting at work—where the fashion staff at the magazine spit out story ideas for yay/nay by the editors—I pitched shooting a video of Anna Dello Russo teaching the world how to pack designer clothes properly, which seemed like just the everyday conundrum *New York* should decode. Naturally, it was approved, so I emailed ADR posthaste to ask her if she'd let us shoot the video with her at her hotel when she was in town. She replied right away that she'd be happy to. One of the things I love about ADR is that she loves being famous and isn't shy about admitting it. Many celebrities who actively sought out fame act like they hate all the attention and we can all go fuck ourselves for caring, which is just ungrateful and obviously a lie. These are the celebs who roll their eyes at you and act like you should hang yourself when you try to interview them *at their own film premieres*. If I were super-famous I would enjoy every minute of it. Deep down inside, most people working in media enjoy attention to some degree, since the work means your name will be made public in some capacity—whether as a byline on a story or at the top of a masthead or as a famous person on the internet. And the second I couldn't stand it anymore, I would make myself seem as scary as Anna Wintour so that reporters would be too afraid to talk to me. Then I could enjoy my notoriety and the enigma of my being in peace and quiet.

. . .

One frigid morning during Fashion Week in February, the season after I first interviewed ADR, my videographer and I headed over to her posh Tribeca Hotel for our packing lesson.

As I contemplated how to dress to meet one of the most fabulous women in the entire world, my closet devolved before me into a pile of garbage. It was as though Hermione came along with a wand, waved it in front of all my clothes, and turned them to a mess of dishrags and tattoo prints. Had I been going to meet a friend from my Austin, Texas, high school, I would have looked at my closet and seen stylish things from places like Zara that look more expensive than they were, but that's because the niceness and coolness of clothes is all relative, depending on who they're worn around. But now, looking at my apparel, everything looked like shit. The American Apparel sweaters, the Uniqlo jeans, even the black blazer I saved up to buy from Saks looked like a one-way ticket to embarrassment.

Here's a dressing tip for everyone with normal clothes who randomly finds themselves in an impossibly fabulous fashion-related situation: just wear all black. Unless you're meeting Anna Wintour, that is, in which case you're probably just fucked all around unless you can borrow something designer. But generally, if Anna Wintour won't be around, wear head-to-toe black. It's a uniform for some fashion people. I think it works because not that many people wear all black unless they're working at Sephora or an airport Chili's, and then it only looks unchic because they have to pair the all black with name tags and aprons. If you wear all black with*out* a name tag and *with* uncomfortable shoes, you will look so fashion, trust. Generally, the more uncomfortable the shoe, the chicer, cooler, and more fashion-y an outfit is.

So out from the depths of the compost pile that was, sadly, my clothes, I fished a bunch of black things: a black blazer, a black tank, tight black pants made of scuba material (a long-lost trend—I'm not doing pants DIY projects with wetsuits here), and stiletto black ankle booties with silver zippers up the front. I wore a black coat on top and carried a big black patent leather shoulder bag with gold hardware that looked like it was molting shiny black bits. I was embarrassed about this bag for about 90 percent of the time that I carried it, including this time. But it was my best option then, so *hopefully she wouldn't notice?*

Suited up in my fashion black, I went to the Tribeca Grand

Hotel, where videographer Jonah said he'd meet me in the lobby. I got there and didn't see him, so I sat on a chair looking much more important than usual, as one does when wearing all black, and waited. At 9:05, there was no sign of him, and we were officially running late. I called him and informed him I was there and ready!

"I'm here, too," he said. "Where are you?"

"In an armchair in front wearing shades indoors. At the Tribeca Grand?" I replied.

"The Tribeca Grand? No—it's the Greenwich Hotel," he said.

Fuck.

"WHERE IS THAT I'VE NEVER BEEN THERE." I began panicking.

"It's not far from where you are," he said, sanely. "Greenwich and North Moore."

Now completely panicking, I ran out of the Tribeca Grand and several blocks over to the Greenwich Hotel. It was the kind of cold outside where the air feels like needles on any exposed skin. Texans were made for these elements about as much as cats were for showers.

Just as I lost all feeling in my face, I arrived at the correct hotel and found Jonah in the lobby. He was acting like this was just another day at work.

"OH MY GOD, IS IT OKAY WE'RE LATE?" I continued, panicking and red-faced, yet also noticing that this hotel was noticeably nicer than the previous one. *But of course.*

"It's fine, it's fine," he said, sanely. "Let's go up to her room."

We took the cavernous rustic-chic elevator up to her floor and walked down the hallway to her room. The door was open, and therein sat fashion goddess/icon/angel Anna Dello Russo at the edge of her perfectly made bed. On her head were Louis Vuitton bunny ears.

Shit, I thought. *She was ready on time, and this is really happening. BUNNY EARS HAPPENING.*

"Hiiii!" I said. "I'm Amy Odell, it's such a pleasure to meet you. I'm SO, so sorry we're a little late." I noticed she had a beautiful black-and-white tutu dress hanging just so on the outside of her armoire.

"It's okay, it's okay!" she said in her seductive Italian-y English, ushering us inside and introducing us to her edgy Japanese assistant. Jonah and I took our coats off and set them with our bags on the floor of her room, which made Pottery Barn's best in-store displays look like a regular barn.

"I brought you the magazine with your interview!" I told her, trying to make up for our ten-minute tardiness.

"Yes, I pick it up," she said. "Several copies."

This, everyone, is the difference between the world's best fashion editors and the riffraff living among them: utter, immaculate, almost maddening but mostly enviable preparedness. *One day maybe I will be this with it,* I thought, in awe of ADR's organization. First, I'd master the art of carrying a smaller purse that wasn't always lined with a layer of garbage and lint.

"Oh great! I'm so glad," I said, going into my standard journalistic "I am so nice and charming, you will thoroughly enjoy being interviewed by me" mode.

We briefly discussed the concept and flow of the shoot before we started filming. ADR showed us the items in her closet—an iconic hot pink monkey hair knee-length Dolce & Gabbana coat, something else outrageously amazing by Marc Jacobs, the couture tutu by a designer no one can pronounce, etc. We decided that she would show us what she brought, with me asking her questions, and then we'd film her demonstrating how to pack these items so that they'd deliver maximum chic-ness upon unpacking.

As Jonah began turning on his equipment, ADR interfered. "No, you go outside," she said.

What?

"Go outside then open the door," she continued.

Okay. She is Anna Dello Russo—best to obey.

"Wait," she said. "This—no." She picked up Jonah's camera case and my embarrassing purse and both of our coats, and walked over to her bathroom, where she flung them onto the floor by the toilet before closing the door. "Now, outside."

Note to self: get new purse, start saving for new coat.

Anna Dello Russo was, through and through, a fashion editor. She had planned *exactly* how this shoot would look, right down to her bunny ears, the dress hanging beautifully from the door of her wardrobe, and, God forbid, the shoot would be messed up by bags and coats that are *not hers*. I couldn't blame her, considering how much my purse offended even me. I wouldn't want anyone to think I owned it either.

We went outside as ordered. I would never be Anna Dello Russo, but I would be her bitch for twenty minutes.

After the door had been shut for a long enough amount of time for Jonah to turn on his camera and position me by the doorway, ADR opened the door.

"Hiiii!" she said, bunny ears perky above her head. And the shoot began.

. . .

I can't say that any of ADR's packing tips stuck with me, but her reaction to my coat and purse made a more lasting impression—I still think about it years later. And if Anna Dello Russo was this averse to my purse during a twenty-minute video shoot, how would Anna Wintour react to everything I own a year later in an even shorter job interview? Allergically, I was certain. But what on earth do you wear to the office of the people who control the fashion industry? These people know the provenance of everything on your person as long as it didn't come from Walmart or HSN.

Given that I now knew only fools wear black to meet Anna Wintour, and that I had no passably chic nonblack things to wear, I realized I had only one option: attempt to borrow something designer. As it happened, *New York* was shooting the spring collections at the time, so the fashion assistant, Eve, who I was close with, had a lot of stuff I could feasibly borrow. She also had a great eye, so she could tell me what to wear and how to wear it. Despite having knowledge of the fashion business, I was still total crap at dressing myself, which is why the idea of me working at *Vogue* was so laughable. But that's the difference between the ADRs of the world and the average people who just end up in fashion. At that time, I had only a vague idea of how to look fashionable, and it pretty much just amounted to wearing all black.

"You need something ladylike," she told me, when I informed her of my epic *Vogue* opportunity. "Come with me."

I probably should have been more concerned than I was about other editors at the magazine finding out that I was illegally borrowing clothes for a job interview at another magazine. But I had been styled in the closet by my friends in the fashion department so many times that I don't think anyone thought anything of us sneaking in there for extended periods of time. It was really just our worktime equivalent of a bunch of girls going into the bathroom at a restaurant to talk about the other people at the table and reapply lip gloss.

She ushered me into the closet, where, in the appallingly expansive mirrors all around us I was ordered to strip down to my underwear.

"Anna's going to know who everything is by," she said. "You have to wear the right label and the right season."

BCBG was afoot, but was it appropriate?

"BCBG does advertise in *Vogue*," Eve said. "But you can probably do better." From within the racks she unearthed a cream Michael Kors shift dress with elbow-length sleeves. It was almost insultingly simple but also phenomenally gorgeous. Seeing as I knew little about what made clothes look good, I didn't quite know if this was The Dress. Though I did suspect that I wouldn't get to wear something as fine until my wedding.

Fortunately, Eve was there to set me straight.

"Yes," she said, looking me up and down. "Let's add a necklace."

She rummaged through a shelf filled with plastic bags full of jewelry and dug out a few Philip Crangi pieces. She doubled a long brass strand around my neck, and once I saw it against the ivory pureness of the Kors shift dress, I knew that this was it—this was *Vogue*.

"What about shoes?" I said, nervously eyeing myself in the mirror. *Also, what if I spill something on myself?*

Fist to chin, Eve pondered my ensemble: "Nude. Nude pumps." I didn't own those, and Eve didn't have any in the closet, so I had to go to Bloomingdale's and buy some after work, hoping the contents of the eight issues of *Vogue* I had stacked in my apartment waiting to be read would magically migrate into my memory as I did so.

Eve-less, I called in backup: my dear friend Tara, who graciously subjected herself to the tedious boredom of watching me trying on unexciting fashion office shoes for forty-five minutes. I was leaning toward a pair of peep-toe nude Cole Haans—another *Vogue* brand, I reasoned. But I was afraid of the price: $250. Tara, like a good, sane, reliable friend, saw beyond tomorrow. "You can wear those again," she said. "You'll get a lot of use out of them."

"You're right," I said. "They're a great basic." Years later, I can report she was right: I have since worn these nude peep-toe pumps to many a wedding in my late twenties. I didn't know at the time that all my vacation time at this stage in my life would be devoted to going to other people's weddings, but I didn't need to because Tara is my seer. It was also a valuable lesson in investment pieces: stylists always talk about "cost per wear." If you buy something you wear only once that costs $200, that's $200 you spend every time you wear it. But if you wear something that costs $200 at least forty times, that's only $5 each time you wear it. (Math!)

At 8:00 p.m., I made it back to my apartment where I spent the night studying as many issues of *Vogue* as I could. There was no point in trying to get sleep because sleeping the night before your job interview with Anna Wintour would be about as likely as sleeping on a *Deadliest Catch* boat. It just wasn't happening. When I finally laid down to rest, I repeated my to-do list over and over in my head. I would change into the Michael Kors and Crangi in the closet as soon as Eve got back from a hair appointment in the afternoon, mere hours before I had to be interviewed by the Supreme Ruler. I would spend the day sitting in front of my computer acting like everything is normal and secretly Googling *Vogue* things. I would maybe complete 40 percent of the work I would normally get done. *I can get this job*, I thought as I rested upon my pillow, mentally reviewing the notes I had made when flipping through all those issues earlier that night. What I did not consider as I obsessed over the timing of my costume change and remembering the names of as many *Vogue* writers as possible was whether or not I actually *wanted* the job. Of course, I wanted it because I was *supposed* to want it. Everyone working in fashion is *supposed* to want to work at *Vogue*. When I was in high school and college and following Anna Wintour obsessively, I decided it's she who I would become. And if I wanted to become her, I'd have to work at *Vogue*. As much as I wanted the gig in the days leading up to the interview, I had neglected to consider the many meaningful ways the job would affect my life. There were several things that I refused to acknowledge as I psyched myself up for the next day:

1. Working at *Vogue* would mean I could not make sarcastic remarks about the fashion industry, as I saw it, with any regularity. I felt humor was a way to lay bare the seemingly antifeminist constructs of the fashion and media industries that drew me to it in the first place. People pay attention to humor. And I wanted people to pay attention to fashion not only for the escapism everyone wants from their everyday lives, but also because it has a lot to do with why women feel insecure about themselves. Fashion and the media that cover it often feel designed to make us all feel fat, poor, ugly, and tasteless. And I wanted women to see that the industry is great fun but in many ways also ridiculous, and, therefore, should not make us feel this way about ourselves. Writing this book as a *Vogue* staffer would be about as likely as the *Sports Illustrated* swimsuit issue featuring only one-pieces and banning body paint.

2. Getting dressed for work every day would be absolute torture. Also, I'd have to do that gross thing where you get Botox in-

jected into the bottoms of your feet to make high heels tolerable, because I'd have to wear those every day. I'd also have to take out a massive post-student loan to afford these heels and other acceptable work wear, because Michael Kors and Philip Crangi aren't exactly stocked in my household with the same regularity as spiced tortilla chips.

3. I'd written a LOT about *Vogue* and Anna Wintour on the Cut, and not all of it was exactly what you'd call "favorable." But once you're called upon to dine with the cool girls in the cafeteria, it's awfully easy to stop talking about them behind their backs, because the recognition—the will to fit in—is at least temporarily more important than the LOL of it all. To this end, a mentor, an editor far wiser than me with boatloads more experience, suggested I ask Anna why she even bothered to interview me. I can scarcely look at a cat without giggling, to say nothing of fashion shows, and I knew she would sometimes call upon six staffers to consider, in all seriousness, how to shoot the clothes in *one* runway collection. How would I do a 180 in attitude and begin to take fashion so seriously *as a career?* Dazzled by the *Vogue* disco ball, I was blinded to the things that interested me most: humor writing and social issues shaping the lives of women. But having spent a couple years on the outside of this world with just a toe on the inside, it was hard not to long to be completely in that world. *Vogue* was the Inside. Once you're on the Inside, it becomes impossible to question it.

And now, as I prepared to try out officially to be a part of that world, the massive amounts of exorbitantly priced stuff the magazine endorsed became a sheer thrill to me. *Yay—STUFF! Eye candy! Pretty!* The models wore designer apparel with such grace. *Skinny! YAY AGAIN!* The celebrities were so delightfully inoffensive and tal-

ented at wearing ball gowns on expansive Sicilian patios. *Photoshop!*
Puff pieces! More skinny! ANNIE LEIBOVITZ IS A GREAT ARTISTE OF
OUR TIME!

And then there were the "issues." *Hillary Clinton! The World!*
Fascinating! And the personal essays: *"I once found my neighbor's 20*
birds dead! It completely changed the way I thought about shoes!" More
pictures of skinny pretty people in outfits that cost twenty times as
much as what I have in my savings and checking accounts right
now! This was *Vogue.* And, like Anna Wintour, she was a classy
broad. A classy broad whom I could then trust not to fan the fame
of a Fergie or a Kardashian or an Amber Rose (though Real Housewife of Atlanta NeNe Leakes and Kim Kardashian have since made
it into the magazine—maybe I'd have a better shot of getting hired
there now). I decided that a magazine that seems to have banned
people who appear on magazine covers for no discernible reason
(and launching a $13 perfume or having a baby at the age of fifteen
is not an excuse) was just the place I should work. When one publicist suggested I try for a job at *Vogue,* I replied, "Yeah, right—I am
mincemeat beneath their Manolo Blahniks." She countered: "But
it's the Bible."

Of course, every fashion writer should work at *Vogue*—people
say it's "the Bible" of fashion, which basically makes Anna the Pope
of fashion and everyone who works directly for her very powerful
and influential. I suppose that if you ever dreamed of dictating what
skirt shape the masses should wear a particular season, working at
Vogue is for you. (This has never been a dream of mine. Owning a
miniature Pomeranian, yes; influencing what people wear, no.)

On the day of my interview, the *worst* possible thing that could
have happened happened: Eve was late coming back from her hair
appointment.

One minute past her proclaimed arrival time, I started emailing her with lots of harass-y punctuation. "Eve where are you????!!! I need to go put on that dress!!!!!!!!!" Eve was my only friend in the office with a key to that closet.

"Running late," she wrote back. "Brazilian hair-straightening. Back soon."

I was still two hours away from my scheduled departure time but felt as though the world was about to enter its next ice age, and I was stranded in a pair of flip-flops. I had a day-terror of showing up to Condé in the outfit I was wearing right then: black jeans, a T-shirt, and faux snakeskin flats. In this imagined scenario, I walk into Mark Holgate's office and burst into tears. He looks me up and down and bursts into tears also. He then sends me home to think about what I've done.

But the thing about job interviews that I'd completely forgotten in this moment but know well now that I have gone on to hire and manage teams of people is that the person you're meeting *wants you to get the job*. This is easy to forget when you're interviewing with people you see basically as celebrities whom you actually respect, but it's the most calming thing for me to remember when I'm interviewing for a job and terror strikes.

To distract my brain from the torturous thoughts of how badly Mark and Anna would judge my clothes and what would happen if I were late, I set about organizing several key items from my hideous molting patent leather purse into a black portfolio-type thing that fit my BlackBerry, MetroCard, money, ID, and résumé. There was no *way* I was bringing the bag ADR felt the need to lock behind a door next to her toilet as soon as it entered her field of vision.

Eve returned to the office twenty minutes later. I speed-walked toward her, hands aflutter. "Eve! I need to change!" I said in my best stage whisper. (I was trying to act normal here, after all.) "Great hair. Very straight."

"Let's go," she said, taking me back into the closet, where I surreptitiously slipped into my "Anna Wintour, please like me" costume. The heels I planned to wear I had brought to work separately, so I put those on at the last minute before tiptoeing out the door for my "eye doctor appointment."

Eve wished me luck, spritzed me with holy water, and waved a smoking clump of sage in front of my head, and I headed out into the world to meet the woman I pretended to be all the time. *Don't fall in the heels. Don't vomit. Don't stain the Kors. You can do this,* I told myself as I hailed a cab. The trip to Condé Nast HQ was so quick that I ended up arriving a stupid twenty-five minutes before my interview. A conveniently situated Gap has never come in so handy. I teetered over there and tried to pretend like I was perusing the cotton shorts selection. I thought sitting down might calm my nerves but with no seating available, I ended up killing twenty minutes by roaming the store like a sleepwalking child in a horror movie, moved by something beyond the norm.

I knew that I'd be warming up with a woman in Condé Nast HR. After a reasonably calming few minutes telling the HR people about how much I love Annie Leibovitz, I ascended to the twelfth floor: *Vogue*'s chambers. Its lobby was decorated in a country-chic style that seemed to mirror Anna Wintour's Long Island house, the interior of which I'd seen on the internet. Layoffs forced Condé magazines to get rid of its receptionists long ago, so there's no one sitting there to call the person you're going to see. Without a receptionist overseeing things, the lobby effectively becomes a windowless living room outfitted in overstuffed furniture, accent pillows, and—an unfortunate side effect of no sunlight entering this enclosure—fake or dried houseplants, which everyone knows are the counterfeit handbags of the interior decorating world. As I wondered if an absence of real, fresh flowers was something Anna had just come to grudgingly accept, several skinny girls in hip-skimming dresses, asymmetrical skirts, and stilettos teetered across the lobby, pushing cumbersome racks of clothes on and off elevators. I just thought, *Glamorous*. But looking back on it, those rack pushers should really be allowed to wear comfortable shoes.

As I waited and people-watched (it's not rude if the people dressed for it, right?), a peppy young lady was being interviewed for an internship. How cruel to interview her publicly. I couldn't imagine doing what I was about to do for an audience, even if that audience was me, the lady with the Personal Styling Disorder. Not that having one person in the room counts as "publicly," but still—I am just made very uncomfortable by other people being able to hear my conversations, which is why I'm so embarrassed by drunk friends and loud talkers. This is only to say: I'm uptight. So *Vogue* should work out for me?

The woman interviewing this girl proceeded to explain the tasks involved in the job, and the girl explained enthusiastically how she's had lots of experience carrying clothes to and fro, and she totally knew how fashion closets work, and she was happy to sign away her social life and bunion-free feet for the chance to organize shoes and earrings while dressed in a very constricting fashion. Because I'm an asshole, all I can think is, *Wrong outfit, not going to happen. Vogue* is a tastemaker, and if you don't demonstrate that you have *Vogue* taste, you're not likely to get hired. This is helpful for the prospective employees in a way because if you feel a sense of doom picking out your outfit for your interview, you certainly won't be able emotionally to handle picking out your outfit for work every day. In addition to her messy half-ponytail and ill-fitting accordion-pleated skirt, she had a big turquoise plastic suitcase, the kind that people push around upright instead of tilted. Having previously been subject to the trauma of possessing the wrong personal effects in ADR's hotel room, I wouldn't dare walk in there with a receptacle meant for holding that many of my things unless it was a Louis Vuitton trunk, and it was being carried by my own interns. This girl was probably one of those types whose parents wouldn't let her move to the city until she had a job, and she was going to get on a train and go right home to Connecticut or Jersey or whatever nearby state she came from right after this interview.

Noticing the suitcase, the interviewer asked if she lived in New York.

"I'm going to move here within the next week! I was just here looking for an apartment!" she explained, thrilled in a way no one should ever be when discussing apartment hunting in New York. It's really the most soul-sucking activity ever if you can't afford to spend $3k a month on a room that can fit a bed and also contains a sink, toilet, and shower, possibly a stove. Of course, even if this girl got the internship, she wouldn't have enough money from it alone to afford living in NYC. Entry-level Condé jobs don't pay enough for that either, which is partly why a lot of the people who end up at these magazines have parents who can afford to bankroll some of their lifestyle, or who have savings or an inheritance or can manage to work two jobs. Because you will also need some good-looking clothes to work at Condé—if you want to work in a place that makes taste, it just seems to be understood that you'll need to exhibit some of it yourself.

Overhearing this aspiring intern's interview was calming, in a way. I remembered when I was in her phase of career, fighting for gigs and my place in the media industry, and mostly failing, and feeling like I'd never get an internship much less a job. Now here I was, on the twelfth floor of the Condé Nast Building, waiting to interview for a position at *Vogue*.

. . .

After the chipper intern prospect said good-bye and wheeled her suitcase onto the elevator, Mark Holgate came out to get me. He is a comforting sort of Brit, and I view him as a rare fashion intellectual—interested in fashion in much more of a cerebral way than a bragging-rights sort of way. From what I gather, he's not in it for the front-row seats or free shoes; he's in it because he finds fashion interesting in the way people find art or music interesting, and wants to decode it the way we are taught to pick apart literature or art. Contrast this with the way many young people get "in" to the fashion world today, by starting blogs full of photos of themselves to show off how they wear shirts. Quiet study or internships that involve untangling necklaces or packing trunks just doesn't take as well with this "look at me" generation. I never felt comfortable sharing photos of my clothes on the internet, so we should theoretically get along.

As a prominent *Vogue* staffer, of course, Mark gets free shoes. *Nice* shoes, too. As he led me into his windowless office, I glimpsed a pair of flashy black Christian Louboutin shoes with silver spikes sticking out all over them sitting neglected in an open box.

"Christian Louboutin sent me these shoes," he said, either to calm my nerves via small talk or so that I wouldn't think that he had purchased them himself. "They've been sitting here because I have no idea what I'm supposed to do with studded shoes."

At this moment I was *soooo* thankful that I had gone to Bloomingdale's and purchased my nude peep-toe pumps rather than worn a pair of studded black pumps I had in my closet already. If Mark Holgate and I have the same ideas about what footwear looks passé, maybe I *did* belong here! Actually, seeing as I still wore my studded pumps, like, all the time, maybe I didn't.

As we talked, the phone began to ring. Anna (or her assistant) had called Mark's office a healthy five to seven minutes before I was due. Mark informed the person on the other end of the line that we were still chatting and asked if she needed to see me now. He would hang up the phone, and this person would call again. "Does she need to see her now? Can you find out?" Mark would say each time. Before we could exchange even another complete sentence, the phone would ring again. After a few of these exchanges, it was determined that I would go to see Anna now. Now? Now!

As I walked down the hallway, I reminded myself not to barf. As if I were a tennis ball in play, Mark lobbed me over to one of Anna's two assistants in the hall. (Maybe she views hiring as a series of matches in which prospective hires are volleyed from staffer to staffer until she slams them right out the door.) She was totally gorgeous and at least as tall as me—and I had to have been six feet or taller in my heels. It was as though she hadn't merely been hired for this job, but *cast*. She nervously asked for my name twice so that she could announce me properly as I entered *chez Anna*. I don't remember how she introduced me, because as soon as we got to this corner nook of the twelfth floor of 4 Times Square where Her Office was located, I was made even more lightheaded by how it looked exactly as every movie or story about the place depicted it. If you're going to Hawaii, this kind of thing is thrilling. If you're going to a job interview, it's a nightmare because it somehow also suggests that all the things you thought couldn't possibly be true about the place are true.

Though I had imagined all the wonderful things about working at *Vogue,* I had never thought about the *consequences* of being so intimidated by a boss—how that affects the work and product you put out—but it must be like the personality equivalent of owning a Chanel suit. It's not necessarily attractive, but it means something to a certain group of people. And to many of those people, it's just intimidating.

The double-wide doorway to Anna's office was flanked by two assistants' workstations that looked remarkably similar to the workstations in *The Devil Wears Prada.* That legendary walk up to her desk was as awkwardly long as everyone says it is. Just long enough for her to stare you down, judge your outfit, and make you feel embarrassed about being in her presence. While the rest of Condé Nast's office facilities were depressingly gray and dimly lit, Anna's were a bastion of white light. Facing her desk were two silver metal chairs. To the left, as you walk in, is a sitting area with a couch. You know it: you've seen it in the *Vogue* documentary *The September Issue* and in *The Devil Wears Prada.* The ceiling in Anna's office felt lower than I imagined, which made sitting in front of her feel that much more intimate and therefore that much more unnatural—intimacy being neither a state nor word commonly associated with Anna.

Anna's desk faced into the office, away from her windows, which looked out onto Times Square and the landmark midtown intersections lit at all hours of the day and most definitely not made to be observed at eye level. No wonder she wears sunglasses inside all the time. But if she faced away from those lights, it means anyone sitting and having a conversation with her was looking straight into them.

So as I approached Scary Flashing Light Anna, she stood up from behind her desk. She was wearing a long-sleeved printed blue dress that looked more expensive than any single piece of furniture in my apartment, mattress included. She reached across the desk to shake my hand. I don't remember what it felt like because I was too busy noticing *my résumé sitting on her desk all by itself.* This woman was not only aware of my existence but *had my résumé in front of her and was going to read it in my presence.* I felt my cheeks turn red as a hot flash settled over my body. Menopause in your twenties: it's not impossible. But lots of urban-dwelling overworked women probably already know that.

As if lifted by the neon beams of light coming out of P. Diddy's head, or whatever celebrity's fragrance billboard was lording over Times Square those days, she leaned forward and extended her right hand. She grinned. We shook.

"Lovely to see you," she said.

"Thanks for taking the time," I managed.

Conversing with Scary Flashing Light Anna requires the utmost concentration just so that you do not behave like a cat that sees a laser pointer dancing behind her head. Half the time, I wanted to bat at my own face; and half the time, I wanted to bat at *her* face. Obviously, if you go into an interview with anyone, Anna Wintour or not, if you treat them like a cat toy, you're not exactly setting yourself up for success.

"So you're one of the people who stalks me on the Cut," she said with a half laugh. So this got real awkward *real* fast.

"Haaaa . . ." I said.

She then asked me standard job interview stuff about what I do with my time all day. I explained that it essentially involved being at my desk all the time so that I could put up a blog post every forty-five minutes and edit posts that came in from other people in the office or freelancers, etc.

"Do you go out?" she asked. "To events?"

"Well, my job is to be at the office most of the time," I explained. "When you have to aggregate a news blog, that doesn't leave a lot of room to be out and about, unfortunately."

"I like everyone to be out, seeing everything," she said. This probably meant events, but also showroom visits, which means going to look at clothes hanging on a rack. Few working in internet journalism in New York have time for this sort of thing.

"I would welcome the opportunity to get out of my chair and go to more events, and see everything," I said. "Unfortunately, that's not my job right now."

For the most part, Anna did seem shy, as my tipster had warned me. She'd often cast her eyes down at her desk and my résumé rather than look straight at me, which could easily be viewed as a sign of nervousness in anyone. I can relate to this. I'm shy and awkward, and the fact that I've ever done well at a job interview goes against everything about the way I am. I suppose the one thing I've got going for me, even if I'm awkward and quiet and have to try so very hard to sell myself when it counts (job seeking, interviewing celebrities), is a conspicuously blunt manner. I'm incapable of hiding my emotions and opinions. I do not know how to bullshit. It does not occur to me, 99 percent of the time, to bullshit. I had no intention of lying in this interview, because I was too scared to, but also, that warning about not pretending to know about tennis stuck with me like the spikes on those Louboutin shoes that so troubled Mark Holgate.

"What do you do on the weekends?" Anna asked.

Luckily, I had rehearsed this one.

"My boyfriend's in grad school in Boston—Harvard Business School—so I go up there a lot of weekends. And I work so much, so sometimes I do work on the weekends. And I'm a runner—I run every morning three to five miles," I said, figuring that Harvard Business School was the prestigious sort of proper noun socialites pepper their conversations with.

"Good for you," Anna said, with a look of legitimate impressedness on her face. Knowing she was a fit woman who put a lot of energy into physical fitness, I figured this was the right thing to highlight.

"Thanks, yeah, I love running. So every weekend, I try to do a longer run—six to ten miles—because it's hard to find the time on weekdays. And I see my friends, of course."

But Anna wanted more. I could see this plainly in her face.

"Museums?" she asked.

"Oh," I began, shocked by the suggestion. *Museums? Do I do that?* "Sure. Sure, I'll go occasionally to see things."

"What have you seen recently?" she pressed.

"Um . . ."

Museums. Whose hobbies are museums? I enjoy looking at paintings and really old furniture and sculptures inscribed with Latin, and I especially enjoy being in really huge buildings that are very well air-conditioned. But I don't seek out places that attract mobs of slow-moving tourists, and I don't make a point of getting out of the house early on the weekends just so I can see the latest exhibits. So no, museums are not a part of my lifestyle—I am the uncultured person who goes once a year when family is in town and we need something to do, because that's what museums are for most people on the planet: a place you go when you Need Something to Do. Like bowling.

I think Anna wanted me to say "Oh, I just loved the recent [INSERT FAMOUS ARTIST HERE] exhibit at the MoMA." Or, "I studied Latin for six years, so I find it so soothing to visit the Roman wing at the Met." And I actually did study Latin for six years, so that was a thing I could have said!

But no. All I could think of were fashion things.

"I do make a point of going to see some things—like the Costume Institute exhibit"—the annual gala that introduces it is thrown by *Vogue* and known as the Oscars of the East Coast—"and I know that *Vogue* has an exhibit coming up at the Spanish Institute, and I'm very excited to go see that." Fortunately, I had gotten a press release about that exhibit today so I made a mental note to ~casually~ bring it up during our talk. Anna, impressed by the reference, looked at me and nodded as though I had just scored a point but also as though she *knew* I was trying to score that point.

"And what are your goals?" she asked.

"Like, my professional goals?"

"Mm."

"I have three. One, to write a book. Two, to run my own online women's magazine. And three, to see my name in print in *Vogue*."

Anna laughed. It was a little condescending, frankly. Like she knew I was trying in vain because I am an uncultured museum-shunning slob who prefers watching *Jersey Shore* to visiting botanical gardens. I tried to remind myself that the person interviewing you is supposed to *want* you to get the job. But I didn't get the sense, when I said I really wanted a place at *Vogue* and Anna chuckled, that Anna wanted me to be The One. It was like she found it cute, the way kids are when they try on their parents' shoes.

"And how's your fashion history?" she asked.

"Not great," I said. I still regret this answer. I think I knew more about fashion history at that time than I let on, but I was afraid of being quizzed. "It's something that I'm working on and look forward to improving."

"But you can contextualize? Decades? Designers? You have reference points?"

"Oh yes, of course," I said only half knowing what she expected of her staff in this regard.

"And do you have any questions for me?" she asked.

Well, obviously. Of course, I couldn't ask most of what I really wanted to ask, like, "Do you like cats?" Or, "Are you low-carb or just low-calorie?" Or, "Do you really make everyone wear high heels?" But anyway, I had talked this over with that mentor of mine who suggested I ask a certain question: I had made a career by *not* writing like *Vogue*—I was sarcastic about the ridiculous aspects of fashion rather than reveling in them. This turned out to be my greatest asset in terms of finding an audience and gaining traffic for my section. So it was actually quite weird that I was here, interviewing for *Vogue*, when I was making a name for myself by being skeptical of many things that *Vogue* recommends and reports on. Rather than ask, "So, what were you smoking when you had Mark call me about this job?" I said:

"I've carved out a niche for myself as, I guess, sort of a funny fashion writer, with a strong individual voice. And I just wanted to know how you see me, as a writer, fitting in here?"

"At *Vogue*, we celebrate fashion," Anna replied. "It doesn't mean you can't have a strong voice or be funny. *Vogue* celebrates great writing and strong voices." What she was saying, basically, is that there is little to no skepticism in *Vogue*. Despite all the skepticism its staff seems to have for everyone who walks in the door or who doesn't fit the *Vogue* mold, skepticism is, amazingly, left out of so much of what it publishes. I am skeptical of *everything* all the time. I think there will be gum in every chair I'm about to sit in, and I can't look at a fringed bra top on the runway without wondering about the designer's ulterior motives. *They want us to look foolish, I just know it.*

"Thank you for coming," she said, signaling that our interview was over. "I hate to cut it short, but we've got Sally Singer's goodbye party tonight." (Sally Singer had recently quit her *Vogue* job to go edit *T* at the *New York Times*. She would later return to *Vogue* after *T* didn't work out. So if Anna likes you, you can't say she's not loyal.)

I knew the interview would be short. I was probably in there for less than ten minutes. The doors hadn't shut the whole time, so for all I knew her assistants were standing outside snickering at me and my pathetic answers. As I thanked Anna and stood up, she walked around the desk to shake my hand. When she got to me, she looked me up and down in this really obvious prolonged way, probably to make sure that even if I'm some sort of museum-shunning, ignorant loser I was at least wearing an acceptable outfit. I have no clue if I was or not, but when I returned to the *New York* mag office after our meeting, one of my colleagues barely glanced at me before saying, "Wow, pretty outfit." So there was that going for me.

Anna's assistant brought me back to Mark Holgate's office. After I sat down, he asked me how it went. "Good, I guess?" I said. I felt comfortable with him. "It was quick."

"It's always quick with Anna," he assured me. As we settled in for him to ask me more questions, that phone of his rang again. He excused himself. He was obviously going to Anna to talk about me behind my back. It's hard not to be excited about (and even more terrified of!) Anna Wintour being this involved in your existence.

When he came back, the questioning finally resumed. He asked me who my favorite designers were, and I rattled off a few names like Vena Cava and Rick Owens—people in the *Vogue* circle of approval.

He asked me why I liked them, and I said I liked to wear them and something like, "I remember Vena Cava's last show—they were doing so many interesting things with safety pins." This was a terrible answer.

"But why else do you like them aside from the fact that you like to wear them?" he pressed.

Oh. God. I did not know. I didn't think about clothes in this way—I thought about the industry that makes the clothes more than about the clothes themselves. Because when the industry is ruled by the papal-like force of eccentricity that is Anna, it's hard not to be. This was when I tried to bullshit—always my plan Z— and did a terrible job of it.

And again, to my horror, he asked if I went to museums. So *that's* why he disappeared—to find out what I was deficient in that he should ask me about again. I gave him the same answer I gave Anna—of course, I do that sometimes, like, totally I do!

"What was the last thing you saw?" he asked.

I think I said some fashion thing, because he then prodded me to name something that wasn't fashion. And I couldn't even think of anything. I could think of nothing at all that was going on around town that I could lie about having seen. So I just said, to my shame to this day, "I can't remember."

Fail.

After Mark, I interviewed with another features editor at the magazine, whose office had windows and whose manner wasn't particularly warm though she *did* offer me a tiny bottle of Perrier. She asked me more hard questions about what I'd like to see done with the magazine, and I had no idea what to say. She also seemed like she didn't want to be talking to me, which made it feel so much worse to be talking to her.

The interviewing took more than two hours. I've had breakups with men I actually liked that took less out of me emotionally. When it all ended, I was incredibly relieved. I felt like I'd accomplished something by trying as hard as I could to get the job. It was like getting off a roller coaster you're really scared to ride but your friends claim to really genuinely want to go on.

A couple of days later, at around 6:50 a.m., Condé Nast HR sent me a rejection email saying that I wasn't quite experienced enough for the position. They were right. I had neither enough professional experience in fashion writing nor enough everyday experience in dressing like not-garbage. If they had hired me, I would have done it well, I'm sure of that, but it would have been an enormous struggle, and I'd have gone on Valium just deciding what to wear every day.

· · · · · · · · ·

Now I can look back on my *Vogue* flirtation fondly. I got a great story out of it, I met one of my idols, and I didn't end up drugging myself to get through the scariness of a job that wasn't right for me. I was reminded that the world's best editors are true experts and in some cases practically scholars in the things that they cover, not just ornaments on the sidelines of runway shows. Not that I didn't enjoy seeing what front-row people look like in their daily lives (still like they belong on street-style blogs). Also, I can go to museums as I see fit, rather than as Anna Wintour sees fit. Not getting hired at *Vogue* led me to Cosmopolitan.com, which I love and feel like I am good at. No one wants me to write earnestly about the merits of asymmetrical hemlines at *Cosmo*, which is fantastic. If I rolled into work there wearing my House of Deréon T-shirt, my coworkers would nod in approval and ask me where I got it.

· 6 ·

Models

Three hundred and sixty-four days out of the year, mail is nothing more to me than desk herpes. Impervious to treatment, it piles up, causing people who walk past my workstation to fear for my hygiene. Only one day out of the year does the mail become something much, much more—carrier of a rare golden ticket to a fantastical fabled thing that will amaze you, change you, and, mostly, make you feel really, really fat: the Victoria's Secret Fashion Show!

The VS show is independent from Fashion Week, and the invite is not just *any* invite. The metallic rectangle is practically lacquered. It's made of such heavy foam-board-like paper stock that once you finish with it, you can reuse it as a cheese board.

When my first-ever invite arrived I RSVP'd immediately. Then I G-chatted my friend Justin.

"i have the golden ticket!!" I wrote.

"i hate u get me one," he replied.

"can't! admits one. bla bla. should i start dieting now or forever hold onto my breakfast pastries."

"go barf in the bathroom IMMEDIATELY."

. . .

"jk jk!"

Roughly 70 percent of the thrill of receiving the invite is the same as that of any other fashion show: just knowing you are Important Enough to be invited. She who goes to the VS show can say:

"I saw Jay Z live, but not the *whole* concert, just his set at the Victoria's Secret Fashion Show."

"No, I can't do dinner, I have to cover the Victoria's Secret Fashion Show."

There's an "I'm in, you're out" aspect to it that gives you bragging rights I won't pretend to be above—although I really wished that Justin could have come because you need someone to banter with you about why the models are wearing inflatable emojis that look like baby pool floats and generally look like the Village People if the Village People were lingerie models. I worked as a fashion blogger for several years before I got invited. One year, a print editor tossed me her invite before my time came. I was so excited—until I saw the bolded fine print about invitations being "non-transferrable" along with some other scary language that suggested armed officers would handcuff, arrest, and strip search any thug assistant who tried to enter under her superior's name.

The Victoria's Secret Fashion Show isn't really a fashion show—it's a holiday-time commercial disguised as an hour-long Vegas showgirl spectacular. Only instead of seeing synchronized dance moves and flexibility, you witness the girls walk, smile, wink, blow kisses, and playfully bump butts with the singers. It tapes in November before Thanksgiving and then airs about a month later on national television. Leading up to the taping and then the broadcast, VS keeps the fashion press busy for months by feeding them every little fact about the production, the costumes, and the diet and exercise routines the models undertake to prepare for the show. The media finds its own stories too, like how year 2010 was the first that an Asian model was cast, which is astounding—a legitimate story—though few outlets really cover these occurrences in any deep way beyond the witlessly enthusiastic "Asian Model Walks!" post. The story does deserve some witless enthusiasm but also some huge glittering question marks about why it took so long for VS to cast an Asian woman.

But this is part of the beauty ideal the brand sells: thin, muscular, tall, and white. It's the commercialized version of a high-fashion runway that freaks everyone out, leads to pervasive portrayals in pop culture of the industry as devilishly fattist, and in some countries inspires laws or other regulations mandating that fashion models' BMIs be a certain number. But trading the weird, asymmetrical black clothing of a high-fashion runway for showgirl-on-crack costumes built upon push-up bras and thong underwear with a side of hair extensions—a beauty ideal seemingly dreamed up for men—prompts millions of people to gladly ignore the reality that Victoria's Secret's fashion shows are no more off-putting than the rest of them. They're just more socially accepted because the clothing and prettiness of the models are things the masses readily understand. If fashion shows are foreign films with subtitles, the Victoria's Secret Fashion Show is *Battleship*, the mass-market action movie with so few words you don't even need subtitles to understand them overseas.

This event is so enthralling because everyone wants to know what the models in the show eat and what they do at the gym so they can adopt these routines and look like them, too.

This fashion show—the most widely viewed in the world—is a bottomless well of media fodder. Yes, it's fun to go to the fashion show and see the bizarre outfits on models in person and watch the world's top pop stars fill in the space around them. But beyond such superficial appreciation of the spectacle, the show raises the same questions beauty pageants or nightclub go-go dancers do if you stop and think about them for any length of time. Once you're "in," you don't want to question the fantasy ginned up by brilliant and aggressive marketing, fantastic costumes, and the world's highest-paid fashion models. You don't want to say what you feel and ruin being invited back again. Access to this exclusive experience effectively blinds many to the reality of what they're witnessing: a bizarre celebration and objectification of wildly hard-to-achieve physical standards.

. . .

The Victoria's Secret Fashion Show has been around since the '90s but didn't become the obsessed-over explosion of glitter and rock-hard abs it is today until around the year 2001, when, according to the *Hollywood Reporter*, ABC broadcast it on television for the first time, astutely realizing that a parade of women wearing underwear stretched to a full hour would get pretty good ratings! In the early years, models just modeled normal-looking lingerie—the kinds of things you'd wear to bed or under clothes but not necessarily just for the purpose of looking glam while wearing nothing but underwear and Halloween costume accessories at the same time. Fashionista.com reported the 1995 show cost a paltry $120,000.

By 1999, the models were wearing wings that weren't wings so much as repurposed neon signs and feather boas on steroids, which is still nothing compared to what the models wear on the runway today, much of which wouldn't fit through most double doorways. The show's transformation coincided with the fall of the supermodel and the rise of the celebrity. As it became more difficult to become a household name as a model, the VS Fashion Show outfits became more outlandish. If no new Naomi Campbells came along to sell the show, something else, like the clothes ("clothes"), had to. The brand later figured out how to make its own stars through the strategic anointing of "angels." It would also assert its own specialness by separating itself from——but still remaining connected to——the fashion industry.

The show used to take place in February, but then moved to a November taping with a December airing, serving as the most epic holiday marketing device of any clothing brand. In terms of sales, the VS Fashion Show has proved a very smart investment. An analyst told *Bloomberg Businessweek* in a 2012 story that the show may cost $12 million, but it "pays for itself." (That $12 million excludes the fantasy bra getup, which cost $10 million in 2013. To be fair, the fantasy bra came with a *belt* that year.) In 2010, the day after the show aired, the chain saw a daily high in direct business, BuzzFeed reported, adding the brand does an estimated $6.6 billion in annual sales. In 2014 Victoria's Secret was named "the most popular brand of the year," according to YouGov BrandIndex's annual study of apparel brands.

What's amazing is how the company has been able to turn what is basically a big Christmastime commercial into a story that takes the media months to tell. And it all revolves around the hot ladies they carefully pluck usually from relative anonymity and pay quite handsomely to model the pairs of Swarovski-encrusted, fur-trimmed, charm-dangling, gel-stuffed contraptions they call *bras*.

The version of VS models' lives put forth to the press seems to go something like this: Victoria's Secret models are born; they're perfect. They have babies; they're perfect. Two days after the delivery, they're getting paid by a swimwear company to be fat free and glowing in their forthcoming ad campaign. By the way, they gave birth in their bathtubs with no pain meds. "How do you stay fit, you insanely gorgeous, happy, life-loving woman?" "I like to do yoga once a week and swim with the baby dolphins off the beach in my modest hometown, where my parents operate a small chicken farm [*Giggles! Hair toss*]." It's mundane. It's mystifying. It's riveting.

I remember looking through those Victoria's Secret catalogs as early as middle school, the days when people still looked at paper pages of things and *called* companies when they wanted to place orders for clothes. (I'll take a stone tablet and a chisel to go with that reference, thanksverymuch.) I thought the women were extremely beautiful—if I planned to look like anyone when I turned nineteen, it was one of them, because these are the things middle school–age girls are conditioned to want—to look this version of perfect.

I was obsessed with Alessandra Ambrosio, who seemed to be the most prolific model of them all despite not getting the most attention in the media (which went to Gisele, probably because she dated post-*Titanic* Leonardo DiCaprio and had abs flatter than a marble countertop).

Alessandra modeled practically *everything* in those days—every garter, every padded disco bra, every pair of sexy sweatpants. The Victoria's Secret catalog then, and now, represented what so many American girls want to be: tan and happiest when doing something as mundane as wearing pink shorts and twirling their hair. Oh, and fat free with boobs.

What I discovered going from looking at pictures of these people to conversing with them in real life is that they look even more unreal in person than they do in photos. These women are freaks of nature: they're supertall and have insanely slim figures yet still have butts and boobs that curve out from their bodies, as though someone stuffed dinner rolls into their clothes. The other thing you notice immediately about these women is their skin and facial features. Some of them actually have blemishes in person, which feels unnatural to behold when you're so used to seeing the re-touched, catalog versions of them. The others naturally have skin that looks like it comes spray-tanned and retouched. Often their eyebrows are twice as thick as yours, as though instead of growing pubic hair they just got a little extra something right above the eyes, because they're #luckygirls. Usually, they're ten times more gorgeous than they are in catalog photos, and you'd hate them for it if you weren't so transfixed by it. I think this means that the camera not only adds ten pounds, it also just makes all of us look uglier. Which is why camera filters that make everyone's cell phone snaps look like Ye Olde Photographs became so popular.

The show cycle typically begins with the announcement of the model bestowed with the honor of wearing the "fantasy bra" in the fashion show. The fantasy bra is covered with diamonds and looks like something from a Carnivale float or one of those stores on Lincoln Road in Miami that sells bedazzled jeans to men. The brand unveils a new fantasy bra each year. The fantasy-bra-wearing model is positioned as the star of the show, and much of the pre-show press revolves around her. In recent years, this "angel" (the term for the upper-echelon of Victoria's Secret models who have long-term contracts and may or may not live in houses made of clouds) has delivered a baby. Take a look:

2012: Alessandra Ambrosio wears diamond bra on runway six
    months after the delivery of son Noah.

2011: Miranda Kerr wears diamond bra on runway eight months after the delivery of son Flynn.

2010: Adriana Lima wears diamond bra a year after delivering first child, daughter Valentina. (Also opened the 2012 show eight weeks after delivering second child, but not in the diamond bra.)

I don't know if VS does this on purpose because postbaby bodies are just so *viral* these days, or if they just pick their favorite model of the moment and many *happened* to have recently had a baby, but a birth automatically adds another significant dimension to the story of the show: *How will she get her pre-baby body back in time?* The curiosity about this gets so intense, so feverish that you'd think these women were picking the jewels off their fantasy bra and giving them away with their answers.

Prior to the 2011 show, Adriana Lima shocked the press with her revelation to a *Telegraph* reporter that she worked out twice a day for the three weeks leading up to it, went on a liquid diet nine days before the show, and stopped drinking and eating anything twelve hours before the show. Her comments stand in stark contrast to many other models and entertainers who claim to get in shape through occasional yoga and never dieting. Her comments also deeply *surprised* the American public, like we all expected her to spend the three months leading up to the show sitting on her ass in front of the TV eating fried chicken and drinking eggnog. But we were taken aback nonetheless because most celebrities claim that looking model-y is as easy as existing (which some would argue is true if you take into account Photoshop). But I don't know why more of them don't admit that it takes a nutritionist, a trainer, time, money, kelp salads, what have you, to look the way they do.

What would happen if they let their secrets out? The rest of us would look like them? No——most of America is content working their desk jobs, avoiding the gym, and never consuming a $12 green juice ever, which, to be fair, tastes bad in addition to costing as much as a dinner salad at TGI Fridays.

After the brand announces the model chosen to wear the "fantasy bra" in the fashion show, promotion around said disco tits and owner of said disco tits ensues.

. . . . .

I was privileged enough to attend a little warm-up event to celebrate these disco tits before the 2010 show, as a writer at the Cut. It was just for people like me, that special species of writer and reporter the fashion industry referred to as "bloggers," though it seemed weird to even make the distinction anymore because practically every professional writer in the world then had to write for something that is a blog. Fashion eventually came to realize they can no longer ignore people who cover fashion on the internet for the greater good of their marketing strategy, but they're even more slowly figuring out how to treat us.

Events for fashion *bloggers* only is something many fashion companies used to do quite often. Sometimes the blogger-specific events take place at the same time as some other more fabulous event, the point being that if you go, you get to watch an internet livestream of the event you've not been invited to. A fancy magazine editor might be invited to the Victoria's Secret Show and After Party while I am invited to a live telecast of the show and an after party for the telecast, held in the upstairs of a moderately nice bar with passed hors d'oeuvres the size of a fingernail (when food's that small, that's what it all looks like, too). It's the back row of not–Fashion Week stuff. One big difference between most of the blogger invites and most of the invites for the other More Important People, it seems, is that the bloggers are frequently bribed with the promise of free food. The non-blogger-specific events are fabulous enough that they don't have to bribe the invitees with food. But that's because the people being invited are fabulous enough that they would never even require a free feeding. And the more fabulous you are, the more fabulous it *isn't* to be seen eating—or at least, that's the message I get from some of the fashion industry's most prominent members, who, despite insisting that they love curvy models and eating bacon, wouldn't want a curve to form on their own figures.

I have considered starting a group called Fashion Bloggers Anonymous, which would bring the industry's lesser members together in a secret basement where we'd confess our least fashionable sins: "I am a fashion blogger and I eat"—looks around in fear—"*club sandwiches.*" Mayo packets and Wendy's chicken sandwich cartons would blanket the floor. We'd forget that we used to approach certain realities of our business—like how so many fashion people are so thin—ironically. (Matter of fact, that's why the Victoria's Secret Fashion Show feels so odd: much like many Serious Runway Shows, it carries with it not a trace of sarcasm or irony.)

So before the 2010 show, I was invited to a lunch for bloggers only at Bobo in Manhattan's West Village, a nice Italian restaurant frequented by scene-y people who wear $300 ripped jeans and have memberships to those gyms you can go to only if you hire a personal trainer. The purpose of the lunch was the unveiling of the year's million-dollar bra, which new mom Adriana Lima would

wear in the fashion show a few weeks later. Adriana was to be present to eat with us and tell us everything we needed to know about
the bra, the assumption being that there is sooooo much to know
about this bra that we would need a whole lunch—preceded by
some passed hors d'oeuvres and champagne—to absorb all of the
information. About a single bra.

When my friend and coworker Diana, my at-work stylist and
top sample-sale partner, and I arrived at the luncheon, we had to
wait in line to sign a release form before entering, which is not a
usual occurrence at these things. The fine print revealed we were
signing away a promise that if we won any of the fabulous prizes
they planned to raffle off, we would disclose the value of the items
and that we won them at the event in any of our bloggings about
them. This made some sense, as the then-relatively new FCC regulations required bloggers to tell readers when they wrote about
things they'd gotten for free. The release also had some other rules
about what we could and couldn't blog about. I was pretty annoyed
at having to sign away my right to free blogging just so that I could
eat lunch in the same room as a mannequin with diamond boobs
and a real-life supermodel, but when I objected, the intern taking
the forms acted like I was speaking Dutch and did not compute. So
I signed and went upstairs. I wanted the interview with Adriana.

Upstairs we were treated to a nice cocktail hour that included
passed champagne and tuna-avocado toasts, all on polished silver
trays. The bejeweled bra was on a mannequin positioned on a special stagelike platform, shining its radiance down on all in attendance. After Diana and I downed some champagne, stuffed our
faces with a few of the tuna things, and engaged in some forced
conversation with our fellow bloggers, she looked at me and said,
"So. Do you want to go look at the bra?"

We approached the bra, which I honestly didn't believe was the real million-dollar thing. I felt like it should be *shinier*. Plus, would they just leave a seven-figure piece of diamond underwear sitting there without a guard? We're bloggers—we *eat*. Can we even be trusted not to get tuna grease on the thing?

"So. This is the bra. Here it is," Diana remarked as she stared at the bejeweled cups, as though waiting for a deep, soul-altering epiphany. Looking at the bra felt like being in an art museum. Not in the sense that it was High Art, but in the sense that I had no idea how to approach the experience. I never know how long I'm supposed to look at a piece or what I'm supposed to be thinking about it to be really *doing* looking at art. But it was not lost on either of us that the event happening all around was like its own fancy rehearsal dinner for this single set of disco boobs.

After the cocktail hour, we were ushered into the main dining room, where a long table was set with name cards, like a wedding or an awkwardly formal *Real Housewives* dinner. Adriana Lima would sit in the middle, with the bloggers arranged in seeming order of importance around her. The more important you were, the closer you were seated to Adriana. I was happy to be one person over from her because while I love being in the presence of celebrities, especially models and *especially* at meals because you get to see what they eat, it would have been terribly awkward for me to sit next to her. Not only because I had royally fucked this up with Richard Gere previously on an assignment, but also because you can't just turn to her and be like "OMG—did I tell you what this guy did to me?" She's not a potential new BFF. You're talking to each other only because you were both *paid* to. Your interactions just won't ever feel any more natural or genuine than talking to your new hairdresser.

After we were seated and began perusing the menu, Adriana breezed into the room. She shook everybody's hands and addressed us each individually, introducing herself as though she were a friend of a real friend. She's the hot girl you want to hate for being so hot, but ultimately can't in the slightest because she's so nice. I was charmed by her because not every celebrity *tries* with reporters. There's a tacit assumption that the reporters are the ones who will try, and the celebrities will fulfill their part of the deal by just existing and saying stuff, quite often little of real interest or meaning. Interviewing many celebs is a lot like trying to train a cat: you make all these soothing encouraging sounds and the cat ultimately is just going to be a cat and do whatever she feels like doing. And it's very likely she'll just blink at you slowly and then turn her head to the side.

Adriana took her place at the middle of the table, and a Victoria's Secret flack encouraged her to engage us in discussion about The Bra, which had been moved to the head of the table (or did it *grow wings and* fly *there?*). Adriana began saying things like, "It is so comfortable" and "I feel so sexy when I wear bras." Enchanted by her presence, my fellow bloggers, drunk on Victoria's Secret/free champagne already, countered with probing questions like, "What advice do you have for women about lingerie?" And: "Are you nervous about the show?" It gets painful. Reporters become so conditioned to behave in a way that will please brands providing them access or ad dollars that many just stop asking the stuff people really want to know about. The end result is that most people in the public eye and many of the outlets that follow them are conditioned to be boring. A good reporter works around this by warming the subject up with boring questions and then joking around with her or asking the things you actually want to know. And the things you actually want to know usually don't involve how the person *feels* to be opening a disco boobs fashion show.

Adriana's nonchalance is halted when the food orders are taken. We can choose one of a few items for each of three courses. When the waiter gets to Adriana, the efficient ordering process stops, as she engages in whispered discussion about her meal. Her lunch was then the last to arrive at the table because she had a special off-menu order in keeping with her preshow diet. When the food arrived, we tried not to eye whatever Magic Lunch Adriana was eating. I tried to extract something interesting from the Victoria's Secret rep sitting across from me.

Over the past three years, some of the top Victoria's Secret models had gotten pregnant and sat out the show; meanwhile, Miranda Kerr walked in freaking Balenciaga—one of *the* great runway bookings—at six months' pregnant. Would Victoria's Secret ever put one of their pregnant angels on the runway?

"HA! Hahaha. Hahahahaha. Haaaaa no," she said, as Adriana cut into her chicken breast, peeling back the skin and pushing aside the baby carrots that came with it. Adriana had had her baby a year ago and was making her big runway comeback this year, opening the show and wearing the very diamond bra seated at the head of our table.

I needed to ask Adriana how she planned to look pretty much as prepregnant as possible by the show's allotted date. Halfway through her meal, a rep asked Adriana to talk to me. Rather than sit at the table and turn around, putting me in the awkward position of standing up above her or squatting at her feet below her (the glamorous life), she ushered me to a banquette at one end of the room, well out of earshot of everyone else there. I could feel the jealous eyes of the fashion blogging community follow me to that booth. This was kind of Adriana, for most celebrities would just have you kneel at their feet and interview them in a posture of discomfort and subservience, a physical symbol of the status difference between the two of you, as if their designer clothes and overall flawlessness weren't enough.

Adriana was radiant, with a slightly shy energy. I could tell as we started talking that she had memorized some things to discuss and really wanted to work in what Victoria's Secret was paying her to say. I warmed her up with some requisite questions about the bra. How was it fitted? She gave me the canned, breathy replies she had clearly thought out before the lunch. "This year they chose the Miraculous Bra, which adds two cup sizes," she said. "It's like feminine, very bombshell, and I think for me, also, sometimes they ask me if I would feel comfortable in it? And I love a push-up bra, so what I like right now is the Miraculous Bra, so they take in this bra and they embroider the diamonds, the gems, one by one in that bra. It's very comfortable, *very* comfortable."

I eased into questions about her diet and fitness regimen. I was fascinated to hear her answers because being a woman who lives in the world I'm trained to care more than I should about being thin and looking hot. (This interview took place a year before Adriana's controversial comments about going on a liquid diet nine days before the show surfaced in the *Telegraph*.) But when the diet stuff came up, Adriana spoke to me like more of a girlfriend than a Victoria's Secret–ordered, thanks-for-signing-our-release-form girlfriend. She explained that she spent two hours in the gym every day in the weeks leading up to the show, and that her diet consisted of only four ounces of protein at a time, and only white or green vegetables, all steamed or grilled, no fat, no carbs. Between meals, she'd have a protein shake or cereal bar.

"Definitely zero carbs for sure," she said when I remarked on the low carb count.

"How does that feel?" I asked.

"Better actually. I feel healthier, I feel much healthier, yes!"

"I could never do that. When I don't have enough carbs I get so, I don't know, tired," I told her.

"Because everybody's different," she said. "That's why I have a nutritionist. I go there, and he checks my blood, my breathing, everything to make sure what's going to work for your body, you know? For me, for example, if I eat chocolate or have dairy, I will feel puffy. Sometimes carbs makes me feel puffy—it makes me swollen. To me? Yes."

And that, my friends, is the difference between a VS model and a normal person. (Of course, Adriana looked about as puffy as a steel pole. In a great way.)

One other reason I will not look like Adriana or her peers, ever, is because I can't afford/don't have time for the nutritionist, trainer, and whatever other assistance she gets (genes) to look the way she does. It's in Victoria's Secret's best interest to make the process as easy and as pleasant as possible for her, because it is largely the impossible dream of what her body would look like now, and a few weeks later on the runway, that makes the brand so interesting and appealing to the masses.

Adriana explained to me that getting her body back to the way it was after giving birth to her daughter was an enormous challenge. Once she started talking to me about the same struggles all women face with their bodies—and how much she *loved* being a mom—she lost her nervousness. "I think motherhood is a beautiful thing. And I think that after I had my baby I feel much more beautiful, I feel much more sexy, I feel much more confident," she said. "I feel like, womanly now, and not like a child, and that's a wonderful thing. I feel giving birth, the experience was amazing. I have no words to describe how beautiful is that moment. I don't [know if] people realize how powerful is this—to have a baby! I mean, you're creating life. I really felt like I'm a goddess. I felt like I'm a goddess! I created a life! And there it is. And so many times you forget about these things." She made me want to conceive a child Virgin Mary–style right then and there. "It's a beautiful thing, to have a baby." There you have it: Adriana Lima, supermodel, felt like an unconquerable goddess when she gave birth, which would seem to suggest that a woman doesn't need all the diets, fancy workout regimes, and diamond bras to feel like, well, an angel. After ten minutes with Adriana, a publicist came over to give me the "wrap it up" tap.

I commend Adriana for being honest about what it takes to look that way at age thirty after having a baby. Knowing that's what it takes to look like her actually makes me realize that I will most definitely never look like her. Going to the gym twice a day and not eating solids for longer than three hours sounds like something I'll never do. I'll keep my cellulite and enjoy my salad dressing not on the side. I am *fine* with not knowing what it's like to be hit on by Leonardo DiCaprio at an after party. (I might feel differently if I were a wealthy housewife living somewhere like the Upper East Side or Beverly Hills, where, television has taught me, life is a circuit of mean-spirited dinner parties, Botox appointments, personal training sessions, salon visits, and lunches where no one eats anything but white wine.)

I didn't win any of the raffle prizes that day—which included a Swarovski-encrusted bra, panty and garter set, and some jewelry. I left feeling like I wanted to have a baby—and bigger boobs, but mostly a baby—along with the will not to eat sugar and to work out for two hours every day so I could feel and look as good as Adriana.

Unfortunately, I already had a blog, which, like a child, is a fussy, needy, and all-consuming thing that not only takes a lot of energy but also might make me gain weight. Sometimes when you're blogging, you feel like you can't even get up to go to the bathroom. One comforting thing about feeling like a much less spectacular human than you did pre–supermodel encounter, though, is that you realize you have no reason ever to look like said supermodel because you will never have the time or resources or need to do so.

. . .

After the diamond bra press palooza comes the fashion show. But before the show, some of us reporters get to go backstage. Reporters here are obsessed with the models' diet and exercise routines. (Unless you're Miranda Kerr in 2011, in which case you're relegated to the topic of breast feeding, which must be a welcome change for her, even though she still has to talk about her boobs.)

You'll find two buffets backstage at the Victoria's Secret Fashion Show. One is for food: hand-carved meats, pasta in dairy-based sauce, brownies as big as your face. The other is for hair extensions: blond, light brown, brown, dark brown. The tables for these disparate sets of things sit disconcertingly next to each other—not that any one seems disconcerted.

"Yeah, that's cute! With the strawberry!" one photographer said to three models posing with the chocolate-covered fruits up to their mouths when I was backstage at the show one year. This treat seems to serve as more of a prop for exhibiting practically glass-encased sex appeal than actual sustenance.

This show is, I'm told, a vehicle of fun and happiness. Escape and beauty. Bright colors and dreams coming true! Sparkles! But mostly, it's a reminder that VS has been inimitably able to put forth an ideal of the female form and that it had a big hand in convincing the world what the best-looking women should look like: tan but not orange, buff but also very thin, glowing but not shiny, tousled yet perfectly made up. It's all very strange, like existing inside a grown man's dollhouse.

Backstage, all the models wear the same hot-pink satin robes bedazzled with the VS logo. Models can wear whatever shoes they want, though. I saw everything from combat boots to stilettos to flip-flops. None of them looked like they *went* with the bathrobes, but this is a strange and magical land where your hand-carved pork loin comes with a side of wig parts.

Some models wear visible tank tops and other clothes underneath their robes, while some seem to be wearing just a bra. Anja Rubik, a model who isn't licking chocolate-covered strawberries before photographers, took one of each face-sized cookie and brownie so she could nibble a bit from all of them.

I was supposed to interview the models backstage and find something interesting to write about the whole thing. Since models getting hair and makeup done while wearing pink robes isn't really a *story*, but their collision with Real Food feels like *maybe* a story, that's what I ended up focusing on. Besides, I see what you people click on, and I know it's anything in the vein of "Model Interacts with/Ingests Food." I wondered if the press were allowed to enjoy the buffet (as I previously mentioned: VERY LARGE COOKIES), but in the chance of limited supply, and because I'm very awkward in the face of uncertainty, I did not. I wouldn't be trapped in this room all day and could leave to feed on whatever I wanted without people taking my picture while I did so. (Is there anything worse than being photographed eating? No, there is not. No wonder so many people who spend their lives in front of the camera become so food weird.)

The food and hair buffets stood at one end of the room. Next to them were a few large round tables meant for dining, like some kind of political convention. They connected to a lounge area consisting of a few stylish, hyper-rectangular gray couches with coffee tables and floral arrangements. It looked like the waiting room of a posh dentist's office. Except for the fact that the rest of the room was filled with long tables with mirrors and lights for hair and makeup. Sitting in front of these mirrors were the roughly forty models who would walk in the show, each surrounded by a small army of people fussing over her hair and face. And in the far corner, created by floor-to-ceiling curtains, was a room with a white sheet of printer paper stuck to the front that read "BRONZING." Even given the fairly fantastic access media gets to the VS Fashion Show, no nonmodels are allowed in here; it must have been a naked activity, this "BRONZING."

Filling in every empty space in the cavernous backstage area were reporters, camera crews, and publicists, all trying to do the same thing: turn this big, $12 million sparkly commercial for the world's premiere mall lingerie brand into a story. It's a lot of work partly because it's hard to find new and interesting things to say about it. And every time you come close to finding a story, Kanye West rolls through to say "hi" to one of the models, distracting everyone in the room and creating a huge clusterfuck around the model about to tell you something really good, like that she can't wait to get pregnant again. I can compete with the *Us Weekly* reporter for someone's attention, but I cannot compete with Kanye West + entourage for someone's attention.

In the middle of the room sat Miranda Kerr, the supermodel who was then married to Orlando Bloom and has a child with him and is the kind of celebrity who dresses up to walk to her car because she knows paparazzi stalk her. She was talking to reporters about breast feeding and how honored she felt to be wearing the $2.5 million "fantasy treasure bra" made of diamonds and other precious stones in the show. She had memorized stats about the bra, like the number of carats it contained and its precise gem-etic makeup. People who are so media-trained are like telemarketers, ready to give the same spiel to anyone who will listen. I am here covering the show for *New York* magazine, and supposed to report on Kerr in particular for a print feature. Since she seems to enjoy talking about her baby in the kind of detail most celebs prefer to keep to themselves, I asked about him.

"This morning I was up at five a.m. with the baby, and then we had to be here this morning at nine, and we're doing, we have a lot of press and fittings and um, you know, it's kind of, it's very busy between, and then we have, like, one show at four and another show at eight, so," Kerr told me as a makeup artist applied indiscernible foundation to her under-eye area, which Kerr examined herself in a hand mirror every twenty or thirty seconds. (Victoria's Secret puts on two fashion shows: one for VS staff and some press, and another for press and everyone else lucky enough to be invited, or so I've been told. Footage from both is what we see in the televised broadcast.) "I really want—ideally, I want to be with my son all the time, but you know, I might as well do this while I can," she continued. "And after I finish this week with Victoria's Secret, I'm going to take a few months off over Christmas so that I'll be able to be with him again."

Kerr said *while I can* because of course she can't do this forever. She seemed to know she was probably on her last couple of years of Victoria's Secret fashion shows, because modeling contracts last only as long as you are young looking and fresh feeling enough to excite the general public by wearing underwear so embellished it makes you look like a Christmas ornament. (The "fantasy treasure bra"—made of 3,400 precious stones, 142 carats of white and yellow diamonds, in case you were wondering—hid the naughty bits of a mannequin several yards away from her.)

Victoria's Secret does not pick models who deserve their contracts just by being their famous selves, the way celebrities deserve endorsement deals. You look at Beyoncé's endorsement deal with L'Oréal, for example, and you think, *Why wouldn't Beyoncé deserve to be in a L'Oréal commercial? She's EFFING BEYONCÉ! THEY ARE LUCKY!* Whereas with Victoria's Secret, you are less likely to look at many of the models and think, *Why shouldn't they star in the Victoria's Secret Fashion Show? VS is LUCKY to have them!* Marcie Merriman, VS's director of brand strategy and planning from 2001 to 2003, told *Bloomberg Businessweek* before the 2012 show taping that the brand "would never pick known models or ones that are already out there, because the brand is stronger than that." It's a vague proclamation, as so many relating to casting models for anything are, but what I get from that is they want people who can fit into the brand and will have to work hard to show that they deserve their contracts. You get the sense that the models are lucky to be genetically blessed, but also that if they don't take proper care of their bodies and their hair and their skin and their image and all that to stay Victoria's Secret–ready, or simply reach a certain age, they'll be out on the street with their hand mirrors putting on their own foundation.

Like Gisele's, Marisa Miller's, and Heidi Klum's before hers,

Kerr's contract ended just a couple years after that interview. But like every good multiplatform celebrity, she has other nonmodeling gigs in the works. "I have my organic skin care line, I have a book that I've written," she told me at that show. "The title is *Treasure Yourself*, and it's won quite a few awards in Australia. It's been the number one bestseller and now it's being translated into nine different languages." The book hadn't yet launched in the United States, she explained. I don't know if this is a line from the book, but when I asked her what's empowering to women—an alleged cornerstone of this excessively bedazzled marketing device—she replied, "I want to encourage women to embrace their own uniqueness. Because just like a rose is beautiful, so is a sunflower, so is a peony, I mean all flowers are beautiful in their own way, and that's like women, too."

Kerr may have been wearing the same pink robe and chestnut hair extensions and bronzer as all her other brunette colleagues in that room, but at least she could embrace her own uniqueness with her very own pair of stiletto pumps. I felt ready to embrace mine by leaving and picking up a turkey club for lunch.

. . .

Adriana Lima was sitting in her hair and makeup chair surrounded by more reporters than most of the models here. Alessandra Ambrosio was roaming around in heels and her pink robe holding a green juice. Models *love* green juice. I've been told some drink it like water. If you think this is a habit you can adopt, let that idea go now: each of these green juices costs something like $7 to $11 each, and I'm not sure you'd make juicing a much more affordable pursuit even if you bought a fancy-ass juicer, picked up fresh produce from Whole Foods constantly, and made it yourself. I heard of one model said to have a green juice addiction so serious that when money became tight she cut back on her housekeeper rather than her juices. This was no small matter since she had no idea how to pick up after herself and was living in a pigsty. And her green juice habit was thought to be a big source of the depletion of her bank accounts since she had, like, seven a day. Meanwhile, the story had it, she smoked cigarettes.

But back to Alessandra: she's not on a liquid diet. "There's these juices right here," she says, motioning to the green liquid in her hand, "and on the first day people really thought I was doing a fast, and I was like, no. I was doing omelet even if it's an [egg] white omelet with vegetables inside, I'm still doing that." (Alessandra, like Adriana, is Brazilian and speaks with an accent.)

"If you're doing the shows in Milan or Paris, you don't really have to do anything besides watch what you eat. And this one you really have to take care of your body, your skin, everything, you know? Because everything is exposed here and everyone is watching," Alessandra told me, explaining that before the VS show, she intensifies her workout routine, focusing especially on her abs and glutes.

"Everyone" includes the live audience and all the people who watch the show on TV when it airs a month later. The VS Fashion Show won't get royal wedding levels of viewership—if the royal wedding is like a Justin Bieber stadium spectacular with enough pheromones in the air to warrant a gas mask, the VS Fashion Show is like an indie band at an outdoor festival that plays at noon when no one's high yet—but still draws around 9 or 10 million sets of eyeballs. As a reference point, the Oscars, which is pretty boring as far as television goes, if we're to be perfectly honest, got 43.7

million viewers in 2014. The VS Fashion Show is really not that different of a program, if you think about it—hot, well-dieted, and well-gymed ladies strut about wearing sequins and hair spray, musical performers do songs—but it's still an infomercial with zero stakes or suspense, so 10 million is actually kind of staggering. Magic Bullet ads *definitely* couldn't draw nearly that many viewers even if they aired at the same time and were hosted by hot women wearing diamonds instead of clothes.

As for the live audience, this is a different beast. Well, actually, lots of individual beasts, but mostly of the same species. You have the press, seated in order of importance, with the "most important" closer to the stage, celebrities in the league of The Rock and Adrian Grenier and Pitbull in the front row, along with a few less-well-known women celebs who may as well not be there since it's not *their* pushed-together breasts and fat-free outer thighs that everyone came to see. And all around, filling in every hole and all the bleachers behind the VIPs, are the men in white shirts and dark blazers, many of whom came in packs, a few of whom have managed to bring a date. They look and smell like bankers / other kinds of people who work on Wall Street. I have been *told* that these men are invited to the show because they have something to do with VS's parent company L Brands' financials and are asked to attend in hopes that they'll rate the stock favorably. (Victoria's Secret, despite my asking about who gets to go to the show, would not tell me. And a lot of the models told me they get to bring only one guest if that.)

The appeal of the event for this odd horde of straights seems obvious—women in underwear, rock star performances, and above all, bragging rights. But even so: this is not a straight haven! No fashion show is! Fashion shows are about clothes and flamboyance much more than the sexy ladies walking back and forth, and this carries over even to something as commercialized as the VS show. Even though the VS show is about some of the models as much as what they wear (which is not true of many other shows), everything glows pink, and no part of the decor that can have a heart or other mark of girliness is without it. Meanwhile, 80 percent of all attendees have such lousy views they won't even be able to tell whether that arrangement of Swarovski crystals on the bras are butterfly- or star-shaped, or whether certain embellishments are made of fur or feathers, so it's not like the cleavage is going to look that memorable. If you take iPhone photos of the show, you're just going to get a bunch of blurry distant shots that make the whole thing look like an aquarium on crack. Also, Victoria's Secret fills the production with so many distractions—acrobats and dancers and Katy Perrys and ribbons and balloons and plastic guns that shoot bubbles—that the boobs and butts are, quite often, beside the point.

Also beside the point: these straights' dates! The women are sparse in the crowd but easy to spot, since they all wear a sort of uniform: tight rayon dresses, no stockings (it's November in NYC), heels that are so high and pinlike that you feel nervous watching people walk stairs in them, flat-ironed hair, tan. They look like the kind of women who dress up for everything, like the gym or picking up the mail. Though the Victoria's Secret Fashion Show invitation specifies "cocktail attire," many people there ignore it.

Before I knew dress code didn't really matter, I did dress up a bit to go to the VS Fashion Show. But then I saw all the other writers attending in jeans and ballet flats and swore I'd never be tricked into wearing uncomfortable shoes there again in my life.

But the women who dress up can't know better. They're there

at the behest of a man, who's either weird enough or out of touch enough or presumptuous enough to assume that the VS Fashion Show is a great place for wooing a lady. It might be, for some couples, but based on what I've seen, it's incredibly awkward. The women dress up to be ogled because they can't help but know they're with a man who is not ashamed of ogling, whether it be her or the BRONZED ladies on display in front of them. And usually these men don't just bring a date but also their gaggle of straight man friends. In my experience, nothing is worse than being the only woman stuck with a group of your boyfriend's friends. Some ladies thrive and really ham it up in these situations, but I clam up and get anxious because I feel like I'm expected to ham it up but really have nothing in common with these people and can't think of anything to talk about with them because I hate the things they like the most (nonleotard sports, for instance). At the Victoria's Secret show, what are they supposed to do? Act like they're really into seeing women walk around in underwear?

· · ·

Backstage before the show, most people aren't talking about the ogling. They're talking about food and diet and exercise. For longer than a decade now, the world has been consumed with blaming the fashion industry for popularizing the notion that being very thin is the most beautiful way women can look, thereby making not-very-thin women around the world feel bad enough about themselves to embark on a lifelong journey of disordered eating, body dysmorphia, and general self-dissatisfaction. The fashion industry is aware of this reputation, of course, and makes a great show to the public of not being—or wanting to be—responsible for this kind of mass self-loathing. We see this in *Vogue*'s "shape" issue, where "curvy" women like Beyoncé and postnatal Gisele get more pages than they, well, usually do. And with the Council of Fashion Designers of America's "Health Initiative," which is a vague set of bulleted directives for designers and others working at Fashion Week that are supposed to keep models with eating disorders off the runways. None of it is very convincing, partly because industry members themselves certainly don't act like it's okay to have some extra fat. You can hardly have a conversation about fashion without the running "no one in fashion eats" joke entering into it—and that idea wouldn't be so ubiquitous if it were entirely baseless. Yet food and diet isn't the main story of other fashion shows, like it is at Victoria's Secret, because we've mostly become numb to how depressingly thin the models are.

Constance Jablonski, a model in the show, dismissed the idea that the VS Fashion Show deserves criticism for presenting an unrealistic body type. "Obviously, we are all real, we are just doing our best and having fun," she told me backstage. "I love sports, I do a lot of sports anyway, so I'm going to the gym a little bit more in the last two weeks, and, you know, that's it." So, no liquid diet? "No, as long as you are healthy and do a little sports, you get sleep, you will be fine."

Doutzen Kroes, released from the confines of her makeup chair and walking around the room, is the first model who asked me how I was doing, which was amazing because most celebrities at any press event never ask about the reporters. "How is it for you? Like . . . the same questions all the time, is it boring?" she asked as she took a seat in a wayward director's-style chair to rest her feet. Boring, no—I could never be quite *bored* in the presence of so much pink and sparkles and tall women in neon wrestling robes.

"I worry that you guys are getting asked the same questions all the time, and I want to ask you different questions," I told Doutzen. "Okay, here's one: What have you not been asked that you wish someone would ask you about?"

"Oh my God. No, I really don't know that one," said the model, who is Dutch and also has an accent.

"I feel like everyone just asks about diet and exercise," I continued.

"Yeah, they always ask what I did to prepare for the show, and I think it's always the same answer—every girl gives the same answer I think."

Which is . . . ?

"Well, working out and watching what you're eating. That's all that it is," she said. "I try to have a really healthy and balanced diet throughout the year, and then I just go really extreme with the no sugar and no carbs two weeks before the show."

"That's not that bad, is it?"

"No, I know!" She continued: "I feel healthy, I feel good. It's actually good that we have the chance to work on our body like this."

She didn't mean, she said, that they're the only people who have the chance to be fit and focus a lot on exercise and diet, but in a way, they are: Who else is paid to do everything they can to look as flawless as possible?

Doutzen has worked with the CFDA to promote its Health Initiative, which I commend her for. Even if their efforts haven't been perfectly effective, they're trying to do the right thing.

"It's a lot of skinny girls, you know?" she said, referring to the fashion business, generally. "Even here, it's like, I think it's important that we show everybody, everybody should be healthy, and there are thin girls naturally. But I think you can see, you can tell when a girl is not eating. And I think that's really worrying for me; I hate to see that," she said.

Does she see it here?

"No, because here I think for Victoria's Secret, you cannot just be thin; you have to have muscle tone. That's why working out for the Victoria's Secret show is so hard. It's like—it's harder than athletes sometimes because you cannot have too much muscle, and for athletes it's about strength, but for us it's about what we look like."

She did not think that VS should put a pregnant model on the runway, though, "because then it's the wrong message. Then it's like, they're not a maternity brand," she explained. "And I think you can look very sexy in lingerie and be pregnant. My husband loved me when I was pregnant. But there's always people that it would turn off, so I think it's good to stay away from that. I think Victoria's Secret's already doing a great job for supporting us and to let us have babies. There's so many brands that would not."

After having her baby, she said, "I was told, like, don't worry about coming back too soon, just take your time and enjoy your baby, and I really appreciated that. No pressure."

Free from worrying about maternity leave was Candice Swanepoel, then a little younger than some of the other models, at twenty-three years old. I started talking to her about her duties as the first model out in the show, and we weren't long into our conversation before her big blue eyes got even bigger and commotion erupted around us. I turn around to witness a throng of photographers encircling Adriana, who was standing on top of the makeup table, robe cast aside, wearing only a lace bra and panty set and posing by angling her butt and boobs simultaneously skyward. Judging by the excitement in the room, you would think she was lying on her makeup table giving birth to a cat.

"Over here, Adriana!" the photographers shout. You have to remember that nothing truly goes *on* back here for hours other than girls sitting around getting their hair extended and Kanye West breezing through to chitchat with a cool fashion person.

"Is that going to be you in a minute?" I ask Candice.

She furrows her brow. "No, I hope not."

I ask her if we're too obsessed with the models' diet and exercise routines.

"A lot of people, it's always the first question: 'So, what have you been cutting out?'" she says. "But I understand the speculation because it is about our bodies and we take such good care of ourselves, so people want to know how."

The de facto way models think about diet and exercise is "taking good care of oneself." Is cutting out carbs and sugar for weeks truly the definition of taking good care of oneself? Or is it really just treating oneself the way one must in order to work for Victoria's Secret in this capacity? These blurred lines are a problem, because women who enjoy dessert and buttered toast in moderation might be fooled into thinking they're not taking care of themselves. They might be reluctant to "indulge" in a whole banana after reading in a magazine that they should have only a half of one with breakfast. The truth is that what many Victoria's Secret models do with their diets and exercise routines is extreme. We just forget it because we've become such slaves to physical perfection that we've forgotten what's normal, what's healthy, and what's just vain.

I don't even have to ask Candice about her specific routine for her to start telling me about it.

"Like me, my diet doesn't really change. I eat a lot of protein; I try to eat more to be more muscular. So I don't know how it is for other girls, but for me, I don't change my diet," she says. "My exercise routine I do. I push it quite a bit ten days before."

She adds, "But certain people question it in a way that seems . . . They want to think that you're unhealthy."

The food and dieting is such an obsession at the Victoria's Secret Fashion Show because that is the *story* for many outlets covering the show. We watch to see the insane wings, the rock star performances (Maroon 5, Kanye West, Katy Perry, Rihanna, Nicki Minaj have all performed at a VS show), but mostly, the perfect thighs, abs, waists, hair, etc. Victoria's Secret will give you only so much information about the show (it won't even tell you why all those straight dudes are there!), so once you've gone over how much glitter was used on the runway (which is often made of glitter, in case nothing else on the screen gets your attention), how much the wings weigh, how many carats of yellow diamonds are in the fantasy bra, the only true arc you have to your story is how the models made it there. And the answer is by working on their bodies—or taking really "good care" of themselves, however you see it—until they have the most enviable figures on the planet.

While these women seem inhuman in their sheer physical perfection, all that diet and exercise suggest that they, too, are as self-conscious as the rest of us. After all, if I had to put on those wings, a thong, a bra, and bronzer, and walk down the runway in front of movie stars and Pitbull in the audience, and the 10 million people around the world who watch the show, I'd stock up on green juice, ban cupcakes and wine from my house, and spend two hours a day in the gym every day for a few weeks, too. But if I did that without their contracts, it would not be considered taking good care of myself. People would just think I had eating issues.

Since the VS Fashion Show is televised, the whole space has to look great—not just the runway—and in Victoria's Secret's opinion, "great looking" resembles the interior of a Las Vegas burlesque club. Unlike most fashion shows, here the audience's benches have nice cushions on them, and the rows even used to be bookended with little parlor lamps.

Being a blogger, I usually sit in the back. I arrive promptly within the specified half-hour time window, not wanting to miss this fashion show as I have others in the past due to tardiness, and take my seat. (Oh, and security is not like the airport: no one pats you down gropily or makes you go through a nudity-simulating scanner.) (There are security dogs, though.) A male announcer with the lilt of a sportscaster says things over the loudspeaker to make us feel special for being there. He constantly reminds us that we're about to see "the twenty-eight most be-AU-tiful women in the world." He might be telling us that "the twenty-eight MOST beautiful women INNN the world" are backstage getting their hair done. Or that the "twenty-eight most beautiful women in the world" are filming backstage footage! Or that if we text or use our cellular devices while "THE twenty-eight most beautiful women in the world" walk down the runway in front of us, we are totally balls out insane and should be expelled. I open Twitter on my phone as the lights go down, a woman with long hair in a tight dress takes her seat across the aisle from me, and the show finally begins.

Everyone Else

THE WORLD OF THE SLIGHTLY FAMOUS
(NOT EVEN ALMOST FAMOUS. JUST SLIGHTLY.)

W here does one wear a fur sandal?" I wondered aloud when I was working at Cosmopolitan.com one day. I had gone from being surrounded by fashion people at the Cut to working at BuzzFeed, where no one understood the importance of an Alexander McQueen corset, and the bright red company hoodie was basically standard work attire. Finally, I was once again in the presence of fashion. Being able to blurt out these questions to people who care about the answers as much as I do made me feel at home.

The style editor sitting next to me, Charles, replied without thinking: "To stand outside of a fashion show."

He's right: you can't wear fur sandals out in the world, where there's dirt, to walk around and grocery shop and have brunch. Fur sandals are for attention and attention only. And no group of people is more down with giving (and receiving) attention than fashion people—probably the only subculture of society who will collectively regard a fur sandal as an impossible invention some-how made possible by a brilliant mind.

The perfect place to wear a fur sandal is the outside of a fashion show, where people lollygag to get noticed by street-style pa-parazzi. A fur sandal can transform an otherwise "invisible person" into a "fashion person"—someone who matters because she was photographed wearing fur sandals. The horrifyingly great thing about being alive now is that it's that easy to be slightly famous. Many personal-style bloggers are proof of this.

In fact, even if you don't share photos of yourself, you can be-come Someone. Just start a Twitter account. Take a photo of a ce-lebrity—again, there's no shortage these days—and put it in your feed. Take shameless credit for being in the presence of fame, and you're basically on your way to having some yourself.

A lot of people who seem to be a legitimate part of the industry have no discernable job. I call these people—who seem to make entire careers out of having or frequently being around wealth, showing up to various parties to get their photos taken riding around in chauffeured vehicles with models and socialites or going backstage at major concerts—Dubiously Employed Folk. Meanwhile, I worked sixty to eighty hours a week to become a journalist and editor, never attaining the same number of Twitter followers as the people who fanny about at parties like it's their job (because it pretty much is, except they're on the opposite side of the velvet rope). And it is an unquestionable truth of working in publishing that your success, tal-ent, self-worth, and reason for being are defined solely and entirely by the number of people who follow you on Twitter. Encountering the DEF, you feel, acutely, the dividing line between journalists and a red carpet, and DEF make it difficult to understand at what point one crosses from one side of that divide to the other.

The result of this social networking is that DEF and a group of people who were once behind the scenes are no longer behind the scenes. Hairstylists, stylists, makeup artists, assistants, lesser editors who aren't "in chief"—all the people we never used to hear from we now hear from all the time. Some people (old ones) call this "noise." I call this the hum of modernity and youth.

I am one of these lesser people batting at the ever-present fishhook of slight fame—only, unlike many people around me, I never expect to be caught and lifted, Mary Poppins–like, onto that sweet cloud of stardom, where you show up and people know who you are just by looking at you and, if you wear sunglasses inside, no one thinks you're the biggest asshole in the room. I used to (and still do, a little bit) feel conflicted about self-promotion. I felt uncomfortable promoting myself on my *own*, but if someone else asked me, I'd be all up in it, no hesitations. I'd buy a fur sandal if I felt like it, and if it got me photographed, great, but I'd never seek out a fur sandal for the express purpose of getting on a style blog.

One day, I was being snide about a certain member of the DEF to my friend Tara over a dinner of brown-rice-based dishes at an allegedly healthy restaurant.

"I mean, what a talentless hack. What is the point of this person? Like, put on some pants when it's twenty-nine degrees outside. Or stay inside for once," I complained.

"It's always like this. In any industry, there's always someone who's successful because they're really good at self-promotion," she said. "Even if they're not the most talented, they beat out other people for jobs or opportunities because they're really good at getting attention."

I realized self-promotion is not only as natural as breathing to my smartphone-wed generation, but also a requirement for success. Though I mostly have always felt weird talking about myself in my Twitter feed unless to share an interaction I just had with my bitchy cat, when the website Into the Gloss hollered asking if it could photograph my makeup cabinet and interview me about my favorite moisturizer, I said yes immediately. I now wholeheartedly accept the attention that readily comes the way of people lucky to work in an industry that is as small as it is navel gazing. And here I am writing a book about my limited life experiences. HI!

Random middling press opportunities creep up on one rather quickly in fashion. One day you're a fashion blogger, and before you know it, the Sunglass Hut is interviewing you for that blog it has that you didn't know existed until it wanted to put your face on it.

You'll giddily do all of these training bra interviews but tell your friends over dinner later, "It was just for practice. I mean, I need to get used to speaking to the media, *right*? My industry is in the public eye so much that it's just part of my *job*." They nod sympathetically. No one will want to punch you in the face when you say things like this anymore because everyone spends all day photographing themselves for social media and a great many getting featured somewhere or other.

Soon enough, the big opportunities will start rolling in.

• • •

Some months into my fashion writing career at the Cut, because my name was on the internet enough, *Elle* wanted to photograph me for a spread about fashion bloggers. It was to be part of then–creative director Joe Zee's column. A Real Magazine! The printed-on-paper, decades-old sort of deal! This would be the most legitimate, sober portraiture of me since fifth-grade picture day. A photo free of duck face that I could proudly send to my mother.

Elle did not assume I was a prepackaged deal who would come dressed to their editors' standards. And they were right: I was about as fluent in looking classy as I was in speaking Mandarin. So I was summoned to their office and led to their fashion closet to be fitted for designer clothes I could never afford that still looked something like what I'd wear if I had style and four times as much money. These clothes were to create the illusion of candid dressing, as though I just showed up to work looking nice like this instead of having barely managed to put jeans on after the gym. This is where I discovered how great $2,000 Stella McCartney blazers look *on*. This is where I also discovered that shoes made just for runway shows but not to sell to people ("samples") are actually torture devices. You truly wonder how models wear them with a straight face much less manage to walk back and forth in them for a full forty-five seconds without falling down.

I was dressed by creative director Joe Zee's assistant, Annie. Assistants, like publicists, make the world go round in the fashion industry. They grease the wheels, style the riffraff (me), make appointments, get coffee, and often do it all in closets or other areas of large offices that don't have windows. To manage whatever emergencies the day may throw at them, they are never without a healthy supply of Post-its and nipple covers. They're also always superorganized and cheerful about everything, because if they're not, they'll get fired and have to go back to working the sales floor at the Club Monaco from whence they came. (Unless you're Lauren Weisberger, and you quit to write a book based on your torture and go on to be played by Anne Hathaway in an excellent feature film.) They have to be humble, because they do a lot of work they won't get public credit for but their bosses will. They might do the bulk of the work on a whole shoot or whole page, and their supervisor's name will end up on it because that's just how it works. The best assistants keep their heads down, work hard, and go on to be incredibly famous and fabulous themselves (see: Anna Wintour, Anna Dello Russo).

While it's true that some assistants document their exploits on reality television or in columns about what it's like being an assistant, many are more focused on having a career than being in the public eye, which is much to their credit, I think, in a business where everywhere you look, someone's Instagramming their shoes because they think their followers NEED to know. And resisting the ability to self-promote at all times can take willpower.

Annie was very much this kind of assistant.

"What designers do you like?" she asked me when I showed up.

"I don't know," I said. I had practically just learned the names of real fashion designers who don't have linens lines at Macy's yesterday.

"Alexander Wang!" I said, partly because it was one of the few I could think of and partly because I knew he made a lot of black stuff, and black is supposed to be slimming.

"What else?" Annie asked as she escorted me to the closet, a big room stuffed with racks of designer clothing. It was like a condensed version of Barneys, only nothing was for sale, and if you take your clothes off in the middle of the room to try stuff on, no one tries to arrest you. Annie seemed to know exactly where all the most Amy-ish clothes were and had packing materials ready to go to wrap up anything I might want.

"Uh."

"I think you'd look good in Stella McCartney. How about Elizabeth & James?" she continued.

"Really, when you're looking at what I came in wearing," I noted, "you can only elevate the situation."

I tried on several black things, including a Stella blazer and a two-piece Alexander Wang outfit: a cropped turtleneck with a matching, equally tight skirt that, worn together, was like one giant sock with sleeves.

You can see why they hire professionals to be in magazine spreads once you try on sample clothing. Giving birth is probably a sexier sensation.

"That looks great on you. Do you like it?"

I looked in the mirror. The sweater outfit was as tight as sausage casing, which meant it was either holding me in, flatteringly, or making me pucker, unflatteringly. I didn't know what looked good or bad, honestly, but Annie most certainly knew. In addition to having great taste when it came to dressing me, she was wearing leather shorts in a way that looked not just normal, but *awesome*. That's the kind of thing that separates a true stylist from everyone else: a stylist can wear shit like that and make it look like something you want, as opposed to when a regular person wears the same thing and looks like a weirdo for owning shorts made of leather.

"Yes, if you think it looks good?" I said.

She said she approved and then packed up all the stuff I might wear for the shoot—including options so we'd have more clothes than we'd photograph. She arrived some days later at my office at *New York* magazine, along with a hair person, makeup person, and photographer. They straightened my hair, coated my face with foundation, and helped me into my sleeved sock. Stylists like Annie oversee the whole process, and I absolutely love them. In making sure their subject looks the best she can look at shoots, they become protective, ready to mess with anyone trying to mess with you. They fight for your hair's honor when a stylist tries to tease it where it's not wanted. They tell the makeup artist to *settle* when she tries to contour your pale skin too heavily. Because the stylist knows everything. Stylists are the seers of fashion, knowing what will look good, when to push you past your comfort zone and when to hold you back from wearing something ridiculous. On top of all that, a stylist actually *dresses* the photo subject. They zip up her dress, cuff her sleeves, pin her clothes in all the baggy places, and they might even fetch you a straw so you can sip your drink without messing up your lipstick. In sum, they're paid to not only make you look amazing, but also to treat you like an infant. When you feel uncomfortable in your designer sleeved tube sock, they'll make soothing noises until you've gone from simpering to giggling again.

I have learned to remember to wear nonembarrassing underwear on photo-shoot days because there's a good chance the stylist is going to see me in nothing but my socks and panties. Maybe they baby people like me so much because, they reason, if I dress as badly as I do under my clothes in my non-photo-shoot life, I must be utterly incapable of putting on my own pencil skirt.

Once I was all dressed up, it was time for the portrait session. This is where the fun stops, if you ask me. I possess a real talent for sitting in a chair while people iron my hair. Whereas when I get out of the chair and have to look fly in the photo, I feel like the Loch Ness monster in a glass display case.

The photographer positioned me at a table with a blowup of a *New York* magazine cover behind me. Some old issues were fanned out before me on the tabletop.

I sat there and stared stone faced as he clicked away.

"Hm. What else can you do?" he asked after a few minutes.

Stand on a ball and juggle bowling pins?

"I can smile?"

"Okay, let's try some smiling."

I sat there smiling. Occasionally the makeup artist would dip in to powder me and the hairstylist would slip in to pet my hair.

"I think we've got it," the photographer said after a few minutes.

Awkwardness, Part One over. Depressingly, this meant I had to change out of the magical Stella McCartney jacket. I squeezed into the tight Wang outfit and was trotted out into the hallway with the elevators. Awkwardness, Part Two: The Sequel.

This is not to say that getting photographed for a fashion magazine is hard or bad, and I don't even say this because I don't want to be the asshole who complains about "wa wa, *Elle* photographed me, life is so hard, boo hoo" because I complain about dumb things all the time. But having gone through photo shoots, I really see that some people are made for the camera, and some people are not. Some people can make love to a camera, and some people can't help but act like the camera is a proctologist. As a professional observer of celebrities and real human living in the twenty-first century, I frequently wonder what it's like to be famous. And having gotten my photo taken here and there, I have determined that one of the main differences between me (probably you) and them is that they do not act like photographers are about to make them strip and probe their body cavities. As much as I think I'm not doing this, and plan not to do this before the photo shoot happens, I have come to accept that it is just part of my nature.

The photographer crouched on the ground.

"Walk toward me like you're going into the elevator," he said.

I obeyed. I now wore black YSL shoes that were about as high as my face is long. Coupled with the tight outfit, I possessed the elegance of a dinosaur.

"We should photograph her pushing the elevator button," Annie said. "Joe's going to want it."

The photographer made a face. "Really?"

I guess he thought it was cheesy, but I didn't know the difference. After all, pushing the elevator button at work is more realistic than me being at work wearing $3,500 worth of designer clothes at one time. That was something I had never done at work, but elevator buttons I had been pushing multiple times a day every day for months. But I was there to do what I was told, far as I was concerned.

"Joe is going to want a shot of her in the elevator. Let's just take one of her walking in, at least," Annie said. "We don't have to use it. But then at least we can show Joe we took it." The best assistants not only do a lot of the things their bosses do, but they can also read their bosses' minds. In fact, this is basically what you hire an assistant for in the first place: to read your mind so that you can enjoy the luxury of not using it for a lot of things yourself. *I've really got to get me one.*

Behind many a great fashion person are many a great assistant. Assistants make sure great fashion people get where they need to get on time, meet the other greats they need to meet for lunch, borrow all the clothes they need for portrait sessions or events. The best assistants set aside their egos in favor of work experience and are unperturbed by the reality that they'll seldom get public acknowledgment for much of what they do. They often know what their bosses have to do, whom they have to see, and what they need for their various appointments better than their bosses. They also protect those whom they assist. One friend of mine who worked for a very famous stylist used to get to this stylist's apartment, where they worked, before all the interns got there just so he could make sure the websites this stylist ordered sex from were all closed. At this job, he also assisted in styling a very famous designer who wanted everything he wore to look old, like it had been festering underwater on a sunken pirate ship since the 1800s. To achieve this look, he dipped socks in coffee and baked them in his oven (these were then worn not as socks, but as gloves). He'd spend a full day running over black leather boots with cars. Did he expect to take a bow on the runway after this designer, because he essentially designed and fabricated this man's look? This man, who is one of the world's most famous designers? No. He tells his friends it was the most glamorous job he's ever had, and that is enough for him.

After I tottered in and out of the elevator a few times, we wrapped.

"Okay, the torture's over," the photographer said.

Shit, I thought. I was *that bad*? I took off the shoes right there in the hallway and returned to the conference room I had changed in, where my civilian rags lay like dirty laundry on the floor.

The best outcome I could hope for was that I didn't look like the raging dork I truly am inside. I had a pretty good feeling this would be retribution for every embarrassing high school yearbook photo ever, and not just because I wasn't wearing metal braces but also because I was wearing a *blazer* in the pictures, and no piece of clothing says "I am a put-together woman with a slick job" more than a blazer. Fortunately, anyone who saw me in *Elle* and read me on NYmag.com would not necessarily know that I roll into work wearing clothes that make me look like a middle-school student, partly because I still wore clothes from middle school.

Ideally, I'd emerge looking not like a slob with good luck but rather like an imaginary, elevated version of myself.

Elle published two photos of me side-by-side that were about the size, collectively, of a playing card. Thanks to Annie, I looked glamorous and rich, which, by comparison, made my office look like a real dump.

Annie went on to become an independently employed stylist. She quit her job at *Elle* knowing that she'd have to just do it sooner or later. She had connections, talent, and knew how to work hard. She has graduated from dressing nobodies like me to dressing celebrities for the red carpet and supermodels for high-fashion magazines and has a fancy agent to represent her. She could very well end up as a personality on a reality television program or launch her own line of bow-and-arrow-inspired bracelets.

* * *

People like Annie who work "behind the scenes"—who aren't in front of the cameras or trying to be in front of the cameras—are hard to find. Even publicists—a job that's supposed to be invisible—get their own reality shows. Lizzie Grubman, who represented Britney Spears, was perhaps at the forefront of the current movement of publicists who practice their own black magic on themselves. In fact, maybe only the best publicists are on reality TV shows because it demonstrates they know how to do their job. Either that, or the whole proximity to fame thing has made them believe it might be worthwhile to pursue the at-times humiliating scenarios you'd think they'd want to try to keep their clients out of.

Grubman got her own reality show that premiered on MTV in 2005, several years after she became New York–famous for backing her SUV into a crowd of people at a Hamptons nightclub, injuring sixteen and initiating an avalanche of bad press and many millions of dollars in lawsuits. What better way to make people forget about all that than by going on reality television, which, by law, makes people look like a more grotesque and generally worse version of themselves? The show lasted only six episodes.

But it continued to set the stage for the culture of fascination with the metaphorical hairdresser to the rich and famous. The fashion, music, and film industries—pushers of "glamour" as the tabloids know it—are most subjected to this. You can hardly work in these businesses and expect to be left out of the scrum where everyone can, and seems to want to, be famous.

A more successful instance of publicist-as-celebrity came in the form of Kelly Cutrone, who appeared on *The Hills* and *The City*, shows about twentysomething perfect-skinned, blond women Lauren Conrad and Whitney Port *finding their way* in the glamorous world of fashion publicity. We watched them sit in windowless magazine fashion closets. We watched them stand next to racks of clothing in Cutrone's East Coast and West Coast offices. We watched them dawdle backstage at fashion shows next to—omigod, the blessed life—*real live fashion models!* Kelly played the part of the scary boss who would accept nothing less than the standard she had set. She was scary because she'd tell you exactly what she thought. She was positioned as a high-powered, easily disappointed workaholic with no patience whose job was, in theory, to clink champagne flutes with glamour. And she'd come at any slightly depressed woman with blond highlights doing a mediocre job in her office like a wrecking ball.

Cutrone had a reputation for calling reporters who wrote about her. I always thought this was a scare tactic, but that's probably because I was scared of her. Once in my early days at the Cut, I blogged a silly item about her being on TV with what appeared to be unusually curling-ironed hair. I treated the "news" as I would any other thing—spent ten minutes writing it, posted it without thinking too hard about how anyone might feel about it, and moved on to the next post. Cutrone was known for not caring about what people thought of her appearance. She's not the woman who spends time heat-styling her hair and obsessing over the angle of her winged eyeliner before she goes to work in the morning. She throws on something black and then something else black, and barrels out of her apartment ready to instill fear and anxiety in whoever slows her down.

After my "OMG in Unusual Move Kelly Cutrone DOES HER HAIR" item went up, my phone rang.

I heard her hoarse voice, laughing. "So you liked my hair," she said.

"Yes, I did notice it?" I replied. You know how sometimes you have absolutely nothing to say to someone and having the conversation with them feels like you're watching yourself live through an awkward moment you would witness from across a restaurant and congratulate yourself for not having? That's about how I felt at this moment.

"We have to have tea," she said through more laughter and chatter I couldn't make out.

"Okay, sure," I said. "Our offices are close to each other."

I got the distinct feeling that Kelly had called me to hear my fear for her own amusement. After promising we'd spend time together in real life, she hung up. We never had tea. It's for the best. I worried I'd have about as much to say to her as I would someone who wanted to talk to me about football.

Of course, I had to encounter Cutrone in real life at Fashion

Week. One season when *The City* was still on the air, she put on a group show that included two of her clients and Whitney Port, aka Lauren Conrad II. Port had launched a clothing line consisting of shiny miniskirts and other stuff that wasn't terribly memorable. Of course, since Port was on a reality television show and the other two designers weren't, she was pretty much the reason anyone, including me, showed up. Backstage after the show, Cutrone arranged the designers of the three labels in a semicircle. Reporters clustered around, eyeing Port like the only free cupcake left in the building. Three cameras hovered around Port and co., ensuring that no dramatic brow furrow or eye roll would go undocumented for whatever episode of *The City* this might be dramatized for.

A brunette who was on the show with Port came up and gave her a hug and said congratulations in such a way that suggested this was *supposed* to happen. This would lend the episode that flavor of realness and emotional authenticity you seldom find at a fashion show. Everyone watching could live vicariously through Port and her now-realized everywoman dream of showing a chintzy clothing line on a real New York Fashion Week runway. When it's all over, you'll be enveloped by the media, but first your friend will swoop in and remind you of where you came from and how great you are without all of this.

Once she was alone, standing awkwardly for a moment that was probably her scripted cue to look *reflective*, I took advantage of her vulnerability and thrust my tape recorder in her face.

"Hi, we're waiting for Mara," she said, referring to Mara Hoffman, the designer, who had been forced into this unfortunate position of having to show alongside Port—who was stealing all attention from the two other designers who, well, had labels that didn't just exist seemingly because they were on reality shows.

Cutrone breezed in with Mara and a distinctly manic energy, muttering her stream of consciousness in such a way that she sounded like an even more intense version of her usual self. *I* was certainly intimidated.

I resumed questioning Port about the brevity of her miniskirts. She reacted as though I had just tried to trick her into saying she hates gay people.

"This is, like, a waste of everybody's time if we're going to do one interview," she said to Kelly, as though I was not a person standing next to her asking her questions but merely a decorative houseplant.

"Are you trying to interview all the designers together, or do you just want to talk to Whitney?" Kelly asked.

The other reporters and I claimed we wanted to talk to everyone because, clearly, if we were going to get quotes from the only real-ish celebrity before us, we'd have to feign interest in the other designers.

I asked how the group show came to be.

"Well, we all work really closely with People's Revolution, and so that's how it came about," Whitney said sassily. She talked a little bit about how she was stressed out by the whole process but claimed her line was doing well.

Kelly, again, like I was unfairly leading the witness, inserted herself into the conversation: "We just started [the line]. This is like her debut and launch of the collection."

Because I *had to,* and also because I felt a bit bad for the other designers getting no press from the *Peoples* and *InTouch*es in the crowd, I briefly questioned Nicole Kunz, who had just presented her line, Nicholas K. She had showed alongside Mara Hoffman last season. "We know the routine, and Whitney came aboard, so we were happy to help her out with the whole process," she claimed as even more attention piled on Whitney in the form of more cameras and more tape recorders and more gossip reporters who couldn't give a flying eff that this had been a fashion show. All it really served as was access to a reality television star who happened to have stitched her name into some sparkly short shorts.

Eventually, the gossip reporters encroaching upon the area like a bad rash became so bothersome that the non–Whitney Port designers fled the scene, hopefully to a Starbucks or street corner where they'd be perhaps even less recognizable but probably more cared about. Whitney was clearly self-conscious about getting all the attention, which is probably why she was so testy (either that, or she just hated me; who can say?), but she eventually accepted that this was going to be Her Moment and deigned to answer my questions. She told me the collection was "*Alice in Wonderland* goes to a cocktail party"–inspired.

She made it sound like she wasn't really planning to have this show—it just sort of happened the way that growing breasts just happens. "You know what? I just—it kind of came into place really, really fast within the last couple weeks when I found out, and I just pulled it together really fast," she said. "But I didn't really think it through so much. I was just like, you know, I have this chance, this ability, and I might as well go for it."

She said she would work "behind the scenes" at some other fashion shows. (But not really, because the cameras would probably be there. If she were really working shows because this was her Real Job, that would be the equivalent of Britney Spears performing at the Grammys and then crewing on Beyoncé's set.)

"No one was with the other designers?" I overheard Cutrone

saying to her staff, presumably the kind who weren't there to be on camera. One of them said something about how something had come up: "Oops!"

Before I could exit the room, a production assistant wearing a headset stuck a clipboard with a release form in my face: "Can you sign this? You were in one of the background shots."

Gladly! Anything to see myself on TV. Because, the media has taught me, I work in fashion, and television—where everyone can see what my fashion industry life is sort of like—is where I belong.

· · ·

The City didn't last very long on MTV. Cutrone went on to have a show on Bravo, but that didn't last very long either. I imagine its cancellation stemmed from how hard it was to pull compelling story lines out of footage of people with small, messy desks in an office where everyone snaps at one another and is stressed out over things like parties and stylists borrowing pants.

Whitney Port is also off a regular series, though she's retained enough residual fame to end up in the British tabloid *Daily Mail* from time to time. I don't remember anything very interesting being written about her of late, but I do know her legs always look nice in paparazzi photos.

As for me, you'll be glad to know I have not signed a deal to star in my own reality show because no one cares about me. However, I did get on *The City*. It was only a second or so of my face on the screen, but it was still long enough for a couple of my friends to text me and be like "omg is that YOU on *The City*?!?!" Fame. It really can strike anyone.

Some people I know who once were invisible people and became fashion people and remain very fashion-famous claim to have grown tired of all the attention. Their stars were born on the sidewalks outside fashion shows, where they posed for street photographers.

Famous fashion blogger Susie Bubble, who moves through Fashion Week with a trail of photographers on her heels at all times and has been blogging since 2006, has an incredibly unique sense of style. She now sits front row just about everywhere, and told me her aspirations aren't about remaining in the public eye or bolstering her image as a celebrity, but she would like to work more behind-the-scenes in fashion, perhaps in manufacturing. "I really am wary of overstepping beyond your capacity. Because you've got to remember the industry is full of really talented photographers, stylists, art directors, and again, we're in this kind of new territory where bloggers are kind of doing anything and everything." She added, "I wouldn't want to disrespect anyone who has worked really hard in the industry, slogged their guts out interning for everyone."

Susie said she has no idea how she gained her following but thinks her success has something to do with being one of the first bloggers to gain attention for her site. "I work hard, but I would say I'm really, really lucky. I'm fully, fully, fully aware that all of it can just disappear in a flash as well. And if it did, I wouldn't be so cut up about it because you always knew that things can go up and down."

Phil Oh, one of the more famous street-style photographers who started around the time that Susie did and came up after the Sartorialist, described the fallout from the fame factory the fashion business has become. "This one editor was always so gracious to all the photographers. Street style helped her career—and she's really talented and had a great eye, so it's not like she wouldn't have been recognized sooner or later—but this sort of expedited it," he said. "People would call her a street-style star, as if that was the only thing she did, which does her and a lot of the subjects of the photos a great disservice. This [past] season she's been rushing out of shows quickly or hiding in a group. I think with an increase in photographers, people get mobbed and people get jealous."

I do not get mobbed. I get my moments in the spotlight here and there, and for the sake of profession advancement, I try to be as much of a personality as seems beneficial. I'll take any scrap of press that comes my way. Like when online store Net-A-Porter's discount site the Outnet wanted to feature me in a newsletter and a video on their site right before I left the Cut. Of course, I said yes—Fun! Photo shoot! Attention!—expecting it to be kind of nothing, but then it turned out to be the most fun shoot I'd ever been on. It didn't hurt that they had a catering table where all the food was tiny and colorful and served exclusively on small square plates.

I got to try on a bunch of designer clothes and tell them how I wanted my hair and makeup done. When I said I wanted my hair blown totally straight and slicked back, they congratulated me on my choice. "Everyone's been asking for voluminous, wavy hair!" the stylist said, making me feel legitimately good for spicing up her routine with a request for a flatiron and some gel.

When I was sitting in the chair, someone came over and offered me champagne, which I accepted. After a red lipstick was applied, a straw was brought over on a tray so I could sip it without ruining my lip look. I would later figure out that they were trying to get me a little drunk so that I'd be less awkward in my shoot. *If only they had lubricated my posing abilities with alcohol when they did that*

Elle *shoot all that time ago*, I thought. Fortunately, though I still felt like I looked stupid most of the time, I now felt I had enough experience getting my picture taken to know not to wear underwear I should have thrown out three weeks ago on photo-shoot day. And that if I looked dumb, the person who got photographed before me looked, well, equally so.

And it was a *serious* shoot, so I was feeling more nervous about it than usual. There were probably around ten people there, not to mention a dense semicircle of equipment clustered before the all-white backdrop. If they were shooting a TV segment on this for *Access Hollywood*, you'd expect to see J. Lo on the set.

When it came time to choose footwear for my first look, the fringed Sergio Rossi booties I wanted to wear were a size too small.

"Maybe you can squeeze into them," one of the stylists told me.

An assistant rushed over with those little panty hose foot coverings they give you when you try on shoes at Nine West, aka foot lube.

"I'll hold the shoe, you push," she said. I stood up, and with one person holding my arm and her holding the shoe I crammed my foot into it. Once I had them both on, I scooted onto the set for the first shot. I was all dressed up with nowhere to go and had to expose my extreme lack of modeling talents to a room full of total strangers gazing at me like a sleeping zoo animal they just knew would awaken from behind its bale of hay and start exhibiting interesting, performance-like behaviors. Sensing my stiffness, the people working on the shoot demonstrated some sample poses for me from behind the cameras.

Once they got that shot, I changed into another dress and strappy sandals. My large feet were now red from forcing them into the Sergio Rossis.

"Oh, shoot, her feet are discolored," a shoot producer said. "Stay there, don't move. Patrick!" she cried to the makeup artist. "See her feet there? The red? Can we fix that?"

Patrick grabbed his whitest concealer and foundation and lay on his stomach on the floor before my feet. He began dabbing makeup on the red spots.

"I suppose that'll do. We can fix the rest in post," she said. "Retouching will always save you, eh!"

I felt mortified. I am not J. Lo, I don't need makeup on my feet, and I don't need someone to lie on the floor to apply it. But having gone from making restaurant reservations for someone who fired me to . . . having makeup applied to my feet while I got my picture taken proved that hard work can take you further than you ever expected. Invisibility for many in the fashion business is only temporary.

I set about prancing to and fro with my faux-surprised face again. I've never been important enough to have makeup applied to my feet ever again. But I'm sure Patrick is this close to signing a deal for his own Bravo show. He had a sparkling personality and affinity for Twitter that just gets you places.

· 8 ·

You and Me

I was sitting next to Joanna Coles, the *Cosmo* editor in chief, in her black chauffeured town car on a Sunday afternoon after the DKNY fashion show. It was September, and Fashion Week had struck again proceeding once more to throw the industry into its biannual period. The magazine's fashion director, Aya, sat in the front seat, and we were on our way to the restaurant Cookshop in nearby Chelsea, where we would talk about Miley Cyrus and eat salad together. I had just days prior started a new job as the editor of Cosmopolitan.com, tasked with turning it into the biggest, most relevant website in the world for Millennial women. This was my first season working for Hearst, one of the world's top publishing houses and the owner of *Cosmo*; my Fashion Week experience was decidedly less dumpy than recent seasons. This is the up-and-coming fashion person's equivalent of being presented at court like a Jane Austen character. You dream of it, you work for it, and one day you realize it's here, and you're out. Just like being "out" you end up dancing awkwardly at a lot of stuffy parties. (Lots of people in fashion dance awkwardly—when people with no fat really "get down," they can't help but look like old people shaking it after a couple appletinis.)

Before landing at Cosmopolitan.com, during my eighteen-month stint at online web then-start-up BuzzFeed, the site known for grainy photos strung into thematic lists with numbers in the headline for people to post on Facebook, my Fashion Week access wasn't so great. Turns out, high fashion is (shockingly) incongruous with "What 10 *Arrested Development* Stars Look Like Now" and "29 People Who Shouldn't Be Allowed to Use Facebook," so my invitations—determined by people who still fax and couldn't reconcile seeing their collection published alongside "31 Dog Reactions for Everyday Situations"—hadn't been terribly fancy or exclusive for a few seasons. And, I realized, I missed it. I missed my back-row access. I missed the community of people I had been with *in* this bizarre world, who understood that Dries Van Noten not only existed but was also important.

Joanna, who was editor in chief of *Marie Claire* before landing at *Cosmo*, needed no one to explain to her why I should go to Fashion Week. She is a sharp-witted Brit who knows as much about fashion as Anna Wintour, but, unlike Anna, possesses human qualities that allow you to actually sit down and have a conversation or lunch with her without feeling like a huge loser about to die by way of extreme outfit shaming. When I interviewed with Joanna, rather than give my clothes the up-and-down, ew-you're-not-actually-wearing-those-pumps look like Anna, she *complimented my shoes*. As soon as I walked in the door for that interview, I handed her a sample lineup of what I'd put on the site if I had the job that day, and she looked at it and said that my first idea—why you shouldn't be nervous about heading into the world after graduation—was "fantastic."

Joanna, a leather-pants-wearing friend of Sheryl Sandberg who knows her way around a fashion show as well as a political convention or pro-choice fund-raiser, urged me to attend "all the major shows" and made room for me on the front row right next to her when she saw me slinking to my assigned second-row spot behind her. In roughly six years, I had gone from the standing section somewhere near Canada to a front-row seat, hip to hip with one of the industry's most formidable and respected editors. The status wasn't nearly as gratifying as the realization that I had physically and symbolically worked my way up. That cliché mom advice is really true: all that hard work and dedication can pay off.

In the car that day, Joanna asked me about my wedding, which was then nine months away. Over the course of a few years, Rick had managed to work through all his issues about my fashion-forward sweatpants and proposed.

"What are you going to wear?" Aya asked from the front seat.

This is one of the first questions women hear when someone finds out they're engaged. This is a question many young ladies just *talking* about weddings for no reason will ask one another. Because weddings are the only time anyone *really* cares about what you're going to wear to an event. It's also the only time anyone really cares about your outfit for a reason other than making sure what they were thinking of wearing was a suitable selection—the main reason women ask one another about their future outfits at all. A wedding is many women's one time to wear something that says, "I am the star today. Bask in my formal wear!"

I had no idea what I'd wear. "You know, so many wedding dresses scare the shit out of me," I said. Devoted wedding dress reality show viewer that I was, I know well that many dresses make you look like you farted toilet paper into a conical pile. The sole alternative seemed to be getting encrusted with so much bad white lace that you look like a dead coral reef.

I vowed to look like neither when I got married. However, given the seemingly dire, antiquated taste level of the bridal industry at large, this felt more like a far-off dream than even a remote possibility. Imagining even what that would look like felt impossible because the wedding dresses that seem to get the most attention are the "too rich to have taste" celebrity wedding looks on the cover of *Us Weekly*. Brides want a dress that makes them feel and look special. Some brides achieve it by wearing the biggest, most eye-catching dress they can find. Others (me, hopefully) achieve it by finding something that's a little bit different from the bulk of what's out there.

"You know what you should do," Joanna said, "you should call up Anne Fulenwider and ask her what you should wear."

Anne Fulenwider had recently become the editor in chief of fellow Hearst title *Marie Claire* after many years at the helm of *Brides*. Well, this was a new experience, riding in a chauffeured vehicle with one of New York's top editors in chief, who had encouraged me to pick up my desk phone and dial the four-digit extension of one of the world's foremost wedding experts to ask her advice. *Maybe I can also ring up Kate Middleton and ask her which tiaras I should buy for my bachelorette party*, I thought. Working at Hearst was really turning out to be the greatest. In order to get this kind of advice otherwise, I'd have to be selected to guest star on some reality show, and I'd like to think I'm a *hair* too sane for that ever to happen.

.   .   .

This was a truly exciting opportunity, buying a wedding dress. Because I am not a regular consumer of Real Fashion—clothes that are incredibly expensive and bear a designer label—it promised to be my once-in-a-lifetime opportunity to have a hard-core romance with a dress I would spend a lot of money on, only to wear one day of my life, for just a matter of hours. For me, and for most women, life is not a series of *Vogue* photo spreads. Life is a series of events that sometimes require wearing a dress, sometimes require leggings and Ugg boots. The life of a celebrity or socialite or model or other regular consumer of Real Fashion is often generously seasoned with occasions where she needs a dress with a four-, if not five-, figure price tag that she will wear for only a few hours. But for the average person, the occasion to disregard costs in favor of glamour, and fuss indulgently over her outward appearance, presents itself only on her wedding day.

And what a glorious time this is. Because there is nothing more arousing to many a female brain than wedding dresses. Whether it belongs to her, her best friend, her boyfriend's friend's wife, or just your standard reality television victim—all wedding dresses possess a cracklike quality that makes them interminably addictive to look at.

Wedding dresses tend to look more "normal" than your standard high-fashion dress. A nonbridal high-fashion show might include sleeves so long they drag on the floor or full face coverings that look like leggings pulled over the head with not even so much as eyeholes, while the weirdest bridal show will feature models carrying parasols. Bridal labels have their own Fashion Week. (Traditionally, wedding dresses are the finale looks in couture shows, so you also see wedding dresses during couture week, but these tend to be weirder and just for show, as pretty much no one but Middle Eastern royalty both can afford and elect to purchase couture.) And separating bridal from the rest of fashion means everyone gets to look at more wedding dresses, totally uninterrupted, all day every day and get as tired of it as of chocolate. And everyone knows "I'm tired of chocolate" is a thing no person has ever said.

(I realize not everyone will agree with me that wedding dresses are this great and some will accuse me of dispelling a very sexist notion that women are defined by their weddings, when they're obviously defined by much more than that, like their careers. And I agree, women are more empowered than that, and I would never suggest they weren't, but I am also unafraid to profess shamelessly my love of all things wedding and bridal because that shit is pretty. And playing with clothes is fun. It's pick-up sticks for adults who have their own discretionary income. It's the NFL game for chicks who don't give a fuck about football. I don't watch sports or scripted television, so I will enjoy very much this vapid indulgence without shame.)

Having spent several years attending runway shows, poring over every high-fashion magazine, studying street-style stars, and working with amazing editors and stylists, I had finally picked up some styling tricks myself. I no longer went around in the same look I wore in middle school. I wanted my wedding dress, of all outfits, to reflect that. I wanted a dress that was elegant, probably with some sparkle, that suited our setting, my fiancé's grandparents' house on the beach. Having spent years writing about the world's premiere designer clothes, I wanted something fashionable. This would be my once-in-a-lifetime chance to spend money on a piece of Real Fashion——a delicious evening gown, with a train!—and I was more likely to reveal my secret alter ego as Icelandic musical artist Björk than wear a dress that made me look like a Victorian-era doily.

My friend with impeccable taste, Tara, who took me shoe shopping before my interview at *Vogue*, suggested I get something like the dress Kate Moss wore for her wedding. I looked it up in *Vogue* and saw that magical photo: the bride, at the edge of the frame, and John Galliano fanning the veil out behind her. (He designed the look after getting fired from Christian Dior when his anti-Semitic outburst was exposed to the world by a British tabloid.) The world's most fashionable woman wore something relatively simple for her wedding. Her dress looked like a well-fitting boho nightie made of fine tulle and then expertly smattered with some glittery doodads. I wanted the same trying-but-also-not-trying vibe of her dress. And the reason so many fashion images seem *cool* and *sort of like something you can emulate* is because the editors and photographers behind them make them seem effortless. But: surprise! It takes a lot of trying. It took me, like, a week of trying to get my picture taken at Fashion Week in some boyfriend jeans and a white shirt.

I began my dress search by making appointments at bridal salons. In New York, booking bridal appointments gets intense. A lot of women travel great distances to shop at Kleinfeld because they've seen it on *Say Yes to the Dress*. This means every weekend at Kleinfeld is like Bridal Black Friday. Good luck. I decided to skip Kleinfeld and lined up appointments at other places not associated with reality television shows.

(As soon as I got engaged, I looked up how to get on *Say Yes to the Dress* but never applied because it looked harder than filling out a form to get into college.)

I was expecting the day to be like the Anne Hathaway smash hit (read: critically panned) film and required girl viewing *Bride Wars*, minus the wars. Champagne for showing up, empty stores except for my family and me, the general feeling that I was acting in my own real-life rom-com. I soon learned that's not what wedding dress shopping is like at all.

At the first store we went to, Gabriella in SoHo, I insisted on trying on supersimple things only.

"I want something like what Kate Moss had," I informed the saleswoman.

She proceeded to guide me through the racks, pulling out dresses she thought might suit me, explaining that patrons were not allowed to pick things up themselves. When you're looking for a wedding dress, you're not allowed to pull things out yourself because when you walk into a wedding store, the assumption goes, grown women lose all ability to pick up clothes and hold them without soiling them, dropping them, or ripping them. And so every interaction with a wedding dress is supervised carefully, like you're picking up prescription drugs in prison. I think this is because the dresses are expensive as all hell and the stores keep only one or two in stock at a time for people to try on, so they don't want to take any chance of a brash bride staining one of them. But really, talk about a way to make grown women feel infantile. After all, anyone can walk into Saks and throw on a $2,000 Stella McCartney blazer hanging on the rack like it ain't no thing.

"Do you like lace?" she asked as she pulled things out.

"I guess a little would be fine," I said. "But I'm not looking for the Kate Middleton value meal here."

When I had enough things to try on, the saleswoman came into the fitting room with me. She watched me take off my clothes while she asked about my life.

"So what do you do?"

I was in my bra and skinny jeans.

"I work in media."

I hopped on one leg and tugged at my pants. There is no good way to take off Jegging-ish pants in front of another person.

She held the first dress while I was down to my underwear and socks.

"At a magazine?"

"Yeah, I work at *Cosmo*."

I was now topless, sockless, and wearing a thong. I tried to angle my butt away from the mirror. If they had given me the champagne I'd expected, this part would be fine.

This is a special moment, trying on your first wedding dress, one that society has taught me should end with a group of women crying. Mothers especially are supposed to cry, either because they're overcome by emotion or because they're paying and it's just sinking in how much this is going to cost.

Am I supposed to cry? I thought as the woman buttoned me in and sent me out into the salon. I just knew if my mom cried, I would cry, too.

I left the dressing room and strode toward the mirror. Instead of bawling, my mother said, "That looks like a nightgown." My sister burst out laughing.

Did you know you can get married in a nightgown? In a bridal store, they slap a $3,500 price tag on it anyway because this isn't only fashion: it's *wedding* fashion. They can charge you something insane because they know you're never planning on doing this again. They're basically silk nothings that you can tie an $800 belt around if you don't want to look like you woke up like this. In my effort to avoid picking up anything that was bridal in a bad way, I had selected only nightgowns. Well, I no longer dressed like a seventh grader, but perhaps I wasn't as good at styling myself as I thought.

The saleswoman went into damage control mode. "How about something with a little more to it?" she said, pulling out a dress with an A-line skirt, empire waist, and sweetheart neckline. I agreed to try it on.

My mother was pleased with this A-line number because it didn't look like a nightgown. But I like all my clothes fitted, and treated the fabric flowing out from my waist like shackles.

"Ugh, I can't move in this," I said as I lumbered across the floor with a scowl on my face. Meanwhile, next to me, a woman was trying on an obscenely expensive Jenny Packham dress (you know Jenny Packham; she makes some of Kate Middleton's evening clothes) with so much embellishment she looked like a chandelier. While I admire a girl who sees head-to-toe sparkle and thinks, "ME!" this woman would have looked better—or at the least, just like a human woman—in 90 percent of the other things in the store.

My sister and I looked at each other with widened eyes. Just because something costs $8,000 doesn't mean it looks like $8,000. Anyone who's watched Bravo knows this. As does anyone who's ever walked into a store, seen something nice, looked at the price tag, and thought, *WTF are they serious?*

Since my mom kept turning up her nose at the nightgowns, which I actually kind of liked, I browsed through a rack of Marchesa dresses (*without* picking them up and carrying them anywhere myself, so as not to break the bridal law about not handling gowns). I knew Marchesa well from going to its Fashion Week shows and red carpet photos of Blake Lively. The stuff is sparkly and lovely and expensive-looking and stylish—this isn't scary fashion; this is the stuff women who live in Dallas and San Diego want to wear when they have a black-tie event. One dress had embellished cap sleeves. But all I could see when I looked at them was the human chandelier next to me. My sister failed to get excited about any of them. My mom kept repeating to anyone who would listen, "She can wear anything."

I put on my favorite nightgown once more before leaving the store. My mom made a face. "I don't see the big deal," she said. "She can wear anything." She held her palms up.

I left the store stressed.

"I hate everything," I told my family. "I'm not going to find anything at all."

"We went to one store," my mom said. "Just calm down."

"Everything is hideous," I insisted. "There's no way I'll find anything I like."

The average bride spends upward of $1,200 on a dress, according to the Wedding Report, which aggregates wedding statistics for US markets. This leads to roughly more than $2.5 billion in sales in dresses a year. For many women—myself included—a wedding dress is the most you'll spend on a piece of clothing over the course of your life. Sometimes we have to settle with our wardrobes, like when you have a job interview and no time to find the perfect outfit. But part of the reason you plan a wedding for a whole year is so that it is not one of those times. The longer you plan something, the more you want it to be perfect. Because your wedding photos are not going anywhere for a *long* time. They'll be on your mantel until you die and then they'll be on your kids' dressers, so it's, like, kind of important not to fuck it up.

. . .

Next was not another bridal appointment but a work appointment. I had to meet Chelsea Handler at the Four Seasons to interview her for *Paper* magazine about her latest book of travel stories. I had read all her books and was a huge fan because she's hilarious and clearly does not give a fuck what anyone thinks, which is what I aspire to as an anxious, self-conscious person. There was no way I was missing face time with her, even for the most important dress of my life. I had been waiting to schedule the interview for weeks, and you don't exactly get to choose the time that best suits your schedule when you're interviewing a hugely famous person. I sent my mom and sister off to find their own food, and went to the Four Seasons, where Chelsea arrived right on time at noon wearing what looked like workout clothes, accompanied by two large dogs. I had seen her host *Paper*'s nightlife awards the night before, and she had her hair in the same pigtail French braids. She had somehow managed to run seven miles in Central Park that morning. I knew we'd get along as soon as we sat down and she placed our drink order.

"Two margaritas," she informed the waiter as we took a seat at a back table, her dogs on the floor beside us.

"With salt," I added.

We were off to a great start. "We stay in places based on how they make a margarita. I call ahead and have my assistant talk to them," Chelsea said. "I'm seriously on the border of turning into Jennifer Lopez. That's what I think of myself."

In my experience, comedians are usually funnier in person than they are on TV. Chelsea proved my point. I hadn't eaten anything yet that day, so the margarita went to my head instantly, which is exactly how I like to spend Friday afternoons when I'm not in the office.

"Two years ago, I went with six of my girlfriends, or six of us in total, and we went to Africa for two weeks' time because I just decided, I'm like, 'You know what? We need to go to Africa!' So six of us went, and we went to Botswana and then to this elephant camp—it's lame, that was one of the lamest parts," she said. "I have never drunk more in my entire life than on that safari, because you are sitting in that car all day long. Not only are you not getting exercise, you are not even walking. You are literally just drinking. You can't get out [because of the animals]."

The waiter came over to take our order. Chelsea asked me what I wanted. I chose a chicken salad and she got the same.

"And another round," she told the waiter. I was drunk. And it was good.

Chelsea took out some pages from the book. "This is me peeing off a boat, in Botswana peeing off a Jeep, my sister and my cousin peeing, Sue peeing." She laughed. "It was crazy."

What was happening right *now* was crazy. I took a break from wedding dress shopping to eat lunch with Chelsea Handler at the Four Seasons, get drunk on margaritas that had been *vetted* by her assistant, and talk to her about books and being funny. What is my life?

Nearly eight years ago, I was getting fired from a job I hated that didn't pay a livable wage, begging for $50 freelance assignments that involved accosting celebrities to ask them embarrassing things, and saving up for $13.99 rayon cowl-neck tops from sketchy clothing stores that blast techno music and look like covers for illegal drug trafficking. Turns out, enough late nights combined with thinking you're a failure while desperately hoping to turn out the opposite can propel you to a place where you're either getting paid to write about peeing off boats in Africa *or* to a place where you're getting paid to drink with the woman who did. Chelsea Handler, everyone.

"Life has become so ridiculous because I have access to such nonsense, and I can go to these places," Chelsea continued. "I've become so infantilized by having so many assistants: people who take care of you and pack you and dress you—it just never stops."

That's the difference between celebrities who wear high fashion and normal people—even brides—who do. When a celebrity needs to pick out an all-important dress or outfit—for a magazine cover or Ralph Lauren fashion show in a park or Metropolitan Museum of Art gala—her options are whittled down by people with impeccable taste. They have access to the best clothing, shoes, and accessories and bring it directly to her Four Seasons hotel room, or wherever she is. Celebrities don't go store to store.

Partway through our lunch, I told Chelsea I had taken a break from wedding dress shopping to meet her. She asked polite questions about my fiancé and the wedding, and the conversation turned to multiple marriages.

"I don't think people should be allowed to get married after two times," she said. "Obviously, you are just not good at getting married, so just date! Why can't you date?! Dating is the best part of a relationship. Just continue to date. For me, I would love to get engaged and not get married. I don't want to have kids."

I lamented the dire state of the bridal industry, and she lamented the dire state of the fashion industry.

"I went to the Met Gala like two years ago, and I was like, 'Why am I here?'" she continued. You know she doesn't give a fuck about fashion—and God bless her—because no female celebrity has the balls to tell a reporter on the record that the Met Gala sucks. (Gwyneth Paltrow once told Australian radio hosts it "sucked"—

but also admitted she was drunk during the conversation.) "I have no idea what the theme was, nor did I care. I knew that I wore motorcycle boots under my Roland Mouret gown. I think it was a Roland Mouret. I wore motorcycle boots. Anna Wintour was like, 'She cannot wear motorcycle boots.' I'm like, 'Well, then, I'll wear them so I can guarantee never getting invited again.'"

Chelsea is completely right, of course, and I knew firsthand based on the specific instruction that I not wear black to my interview with her. The Met Gala is an absurd cavalcade of famous people wearing things so *fashionable* that you can hardly conceive of them as anything but holiday window displays that occasionally resemble a dress. Working inside the industry, forgetting this is easy because fashion devotees treat attending the Met Gala like sitting on the front row, times 100 trillion. If there are negative-row fashion show seats, they're Met Gala tickets.

Three margaritas deep, I stumbled back onto Fifty-Seventh Street and started weaving my way down the sidewalk to the Monique Lhuillier boutique.

"Jst finishd w Chelsee," I texted my sister. "B there in a sex."

When I arrived at the store, I was in a much better mood than I had been when I left. "Sorry. I think I am late," I said to the saleswoman. She looked busy.

"You are, but you still have forty-five minutes. I can't give you the full hour because it's a trunk show and we're booked solid."

Trunk show. A trunk show has zero things to do with trunks and instead is a fancy way of saying, you get 15 percent off on anything you buy that day.

"What are you looking for?" she asked.

"I just want something," I said as we climbed a beautiful staircase to the dresses on the second floor, "sssimple."

She proceeded to pull things from the racks. "You know the Kate Moss thing she wore," I said. I turned to my mom and sister. "I had three margaritas."

My mother closed her eyes and raised her eyebrows.

Most of the dresses here were strapless and lacy. I had a big room with its own pedestal for me to stand on and huge mirrors and girly moldings that made me feel like I was in my own private dollhouse. It was so big my mom and sister could sit in here with me, so I really had an audience for getting naked again. But three margs in, I didn't even care if the door was closed.

"Oh, I like this one," I said when I put on a plain strapless ivory lace sheath dress with a little gold shimmer to it. "This is pretty." Things were seemingly looking up. This lace, by some miracle, didn't look like salt crusts.

The saleswoman tied a sparkly belt around my waist. "You can wear it like this or you can wear it plain," she said. I would learn during wedding dress shopping that every accessory you buy for a dress from a bridal designer often adds another $1,000. Even if it's a piece of ribbon with some rhinestones on it or a piece of tulle with a comb attached to it (veil). Because bridal designers know that if you've ended up in a store with $12,000 gowns hanging on the racks, whether that's your budget or not, you've probably grown up watching red carpet preshows and beauty pageants knowing that your only moment for similar glamour would be your wedding day, so you'll suck it up and spend whatever you feel like you need to.

Standing there, drunk, in this pretty lace dress, I could see it. I could see myself getting married in this. My mom and sister agreed it was pretty. Other brides in the store regarded me and told their salespeople they wanted to try it on, too. I felt like a sensation.

Then again, you never know what's truly happening around you when you're drunk in the middle of the day.

We wrote down the details of the lace dress and went to our next appointment at a store that bills itself as being for an "alternative bride," which I won't go into detail about except to say one of my fashion editor friends says, "It's like Etsy threw up in there," and I wouldn't disagree with her.

That evening we went out to dinner with my fiancé, where I ordered him to guess how I fared that day.

"I'm guessing you didn't find a dress," he said.

"I hated everything," I said. "Bridal is terrible. I'll have to marry you in a bed sheet and a belt. I'll look like the Little Mermaid washed up without her fish tail."

"What? I thought you liked the Monique Lhuillier," my sister said.

"I don't anymore. I hated everything," I said.

"You seemed like you liked it in the store. You were going on and on about how pretty that lace dress was."

"Well, I had just had some margaritas," I said. "That's why."

"I knew that would happen," my mom said. "I knew she'd have lunch with Chelsea, get drunk, and then find something she likes. So much for that."

I had one more day to find a dress before my mom and sister left town. I obviously couldn't do this without them. There's a reason women have to bring their families to shop with them for a wedding dress, and that's because their friends would never have the patience for it.

The next morning, we rose early and went to fashion's Upper East Side mecca: Bergdorf Goodman. I can't say enough good things about the Bergdorf Goodman bridal salon. It's like being inside of a cupcake. Every girly dream comes true in the Bergdorf Goodman bridal salon!

"You only have an hour," the saleswoman informed us. "No longer. We have appointments all day."

An hour sounds like a long time, but you could really spend three hours in there trying on everything. All the dresses are insanely gorgeous. I pulled at least fifteen from the racks for the first round.

Suddenly everything seemed like a possibility. I was living out the montage in the *Sex and the City* movie where Sarah Jessica Parker tries on a million dresses for her *Vogue* bridal shoot, only the dresses were things people actually wear in real life as opposed to—fabulous though they were—dresses with sleeves made of queen-sized duvets.

Boosting my ego (as though I needed it) was every salesperson in the store, who would compliment me every time I left my room.

One of the first dresses I tried on was a Monique Lhuillier creation I hadn't noticed in her store, consisting of a beautiful embellished bodice and an A-line tulle skirt.

"I love this," I proclaimed.

"How much is it?" my mom asked.

"This is twelve thousand dollars," the saleswoman said.

"Forget it," my mom replied.

"Never mind, I hate it," I lied to myself.

When I put on one dress by the designer Ines Di Santo, a strapless mermaid gown with lace appliqué, the saleswoman helping me blurted out, "I will get the designer. She is here today! Stay here."

Ines di Santo, who, incidentally, made my sister's wedding dress, was there doing a trunk show. Along with a discount, this meant she was there in person to upsell her wares and fuss over you. She had long bleached-blond hair worn to one side in a cascade of big curls, immaculate red lips, and kohl-lined eyes, and spoke with an Italian accent.

"Oh my God. Stunning. That looks stunning on you," she said as she entered my Bergdorf boudoir. "Who is here? Is this Mom?"

"Yes, that's my mom, Gail. And that's my sister, Holly, who got married in one of your dresses!!!" I was more excited about my sister coming into contact with this woman than myself. Because somehow a woman actually meeting the person responsible for the most epic dress of her life feels like the Destiny's Child reunion we've all been waiting for only it happens right in front of your face.

"I wish I had a picture," my sister said, but she is older than me and got married back when camera phones weren't a thing.

"I have other things you must try. Come," she said, and led me out into the front of the bridal salon, where her collection was on prominent display.

"You like lace? You must try this; it's very beautiful," she said, pulling samples from the rack for the saleswoman to take to my boudoir. "You can wear this, not everyone," she said, pulling a spaghetti-strap lace piece with a slight shimmer to it. "And this, this is a mermaid—very dramatic." She pulled a pretty dress with a mass of tulle dangling from the bottom. Either she does this for every bride she catches trying on one of her dresses or this is what it feels like to be a muse.

I tried on the shimmering lace dress next. It was sexy in a way that would be great for a different situation—let's say, like not wearing it in front of your mom. It had a split neckline that plunged in the front almost to the navel and a slit in the front that came up past the knee. Since it was a runway sample, it fit like Saran Wrap.

"This one is sexy. Very *wow*," said Ines, as she led me around the salon.

It did look kind of amazing but also amazingly nude. If I wanted to give off the *illusion* of wearing clothing at my wedding rather than unmistakably being clothed, this was the dress for me.

"What does Mom think?" the saleswoman asked when we returned to our room.

"Well," she began. "It's not really for me."

"A little too sexy for Mom? Haha. Okay, let's try the next one."

Next was the dress with the mermaid tulle bottom so massive it allowed the dress to stand upright on the floor. This made for relatively easy dressing but nearly impossible walking.

"I'm not sure if I can walk in this," I told the saleswoman. She gave me her hand and helped me off the pedestal. Ines took my hand and led me out of the door and around the floor.

"This also looks great. How do you feel? What do you think?"

"Well, it's very pretty, but I think I'm going to need to be able to walk, and I'm not sure this is *great* for that."

I didn't want to say anything negative about her dresses because I was determined to be a good one-hour muse. "Come here; you can go out," she said, holding my hand as she led me out of the salon and into the home goods area, where there was another large mirror. My sister and mom were following me. I saw a look of horror creep into my sister's eyes as I realized my tulle base was close to knocking a large decorative bowl that probably cost as much as the dress off a small glass table.

"Careful!" she cried. Freaked out, I hustled back into the bridal salon as fast as my six-foot tulle base would travel. In what felt like five minutes, our time in the fairy-tale wonderland that is the Bergdorf Goodman bridal salon was up. We had a few strong options, which the saleswoman wrote down on fine stationary. It was time to exit this heavenly, heavenly place and return to my very basic existence.

I left experiencing a surge of endorphins from the sheer knowledge that I would not, after all, have to get married in a very expensive nightgown. And if I was going to spend a lot of money on this dress, it needed to be *spectacular*, not just a slip with a train and a lining. Some wedding dresses are actually wedding-y in a good way! And they're all hiding in one of the world's most expensive stores, what do you know.

.   .   .

We went to the Reem Acra showroom next. And as I was learning during my dress search, something truly special is happening when you're looking for an outfit in not a store but a showroom with no storefront because the shit they sell is so expensive, so fine, so otherworldly that you have to make an appointment to be in its presence. The Acra showroom is on the second floor of a large office building on Fifth Avenue just below Fifty-Seventh Street. The building's interior is gray and unremarkable, but when you walk into the showroom, you're treated to a relaxing water feature and soothing video footage of the latest Reem Acra runway show. Past the entry area are two huge rooms filled with the most beautiful gowns you've ever seen in your life. Tulle and lace and sparkle create a dazzling haven of femininity and happiness while instilling in all who enter a deep-seated anxiety that they should either wash their hands immediately or wrap themselves entirely in latex before proceeding.

A blond sales associate led us through the floor. I told her I wanted something simple and fitted with a splash of lace or spar-kle. She went immediately to what looked like kind of an unre-markable off-white rag hanging limply from a rack.

"This is a runway sample, so it's not in the best condition, but it's simple with a little lace and a nice little train," she said, holding out the dress. I agreed to try it. I pulled out several more dresses with statement cap sleeves in rhinestones or lace and a Cinderella dress with a smattering of silver sequins over the bodice and a full, floaty skirt.

"That's not the style you were looking for," my sister pointed out.

"I know, but Mom won't say it looks like a nightgown," I told her. Besides, I'll probably never have another reason to put on a dress like that. It's not like I'm Amy Adams in *Enchanted* (unfortu-nately). Besides, even the most cynical, stone-hearted New York media people like myself get emotional and excited around inani-mate objects of fashion, especially when sequins are involved.

The sales associate came into the dressing room with me, which meant another hour of stripping down to panties in front of a stranger. But at this point, so many people in New York City had seen me in nothing but nude thong underwear that it felt as natural as a handshake. The first dress I put on was the raglike runway sample. Lace cascaded asymmetrically down the front of the bod-ice and dripped over invisible illusion tulle netting. The back was low-cut. It was fitted through the bodice and had a small train.

Being a runway sample, the dress was *tight*. Like compression-stocking tight. Fortunately, it was already a little ripped, so if moving caused it to burst open, they probably wouldn't force me to buy it. I walked out into the store to look at myself in a full-length mirror.

I cocked my head to one side. This dress, why, this dress was something special. This dress wasn't like all the others that acted like they'd be all great on the hanger and then got me out of my pants only to roll over and fall asleep as soon as I let them have their way with me. No, this dress was different. This dress would call me the next day. This dress would hold the door open for me and insist on buying me dinner. This dress was maybe actually, really, finally, the *one*.

"I think—" I began, my mom and sister looking on intently, hoping, no doubt, that this tedious ordeal of watching me try on so much white stuff was finally about to end. "I think I love it."

"What?!" My sister recoiled.

"Well, I haven't heard that all day," my mom said.

"No, I do—I think I love this dress!"

"Do you want to try the veil?" the saleswoman asked. (*Obviously.*)

She stuck it into my hair with a small comb. "It has just a touch of the same lace that's in the dress."

The veil was long and dramatic, made from the lightest sheer tulle and trimmed on the sides with lace. I couldn't believe I ever considered not having a veil. Veils are everything! Trying on veils is actually more fun than trying on the dresses because veils are what make you look like an actual bride as opposed to a person who's overdressed. I started walking around in circles just to see the veil swirl around me. My mom dutifully documented me with her camera phone. Trying on wedding dresses is apparently the grown adult's version of a piano recital. She'll never feel like videotaping me this much ever again in my life.

As I sashayed to and fro in my dress, negotiating the train, admiring the frothy veil swirling about me, a petite, well-groomed blonde carrying a Longchamp bag entered the showroom.

"I've been to eighteen stores," she told her sales associate. "My six bridesmaids have all come with me. But I just can't find anything. So I was like, I just have to go by myself. I was here last week, but I just needed to clear my head and come back alone."

Oh my God. My eyes widened. *She made six people do this with her? Over the course of eighteen stores?* If you try on seven dresses in each place, that's 126 dresses. *This woman has been through more than a hundred dresses and still hasn't found something.*

I returned to my room to change into the Cinderella dress with the sequins. This was also divine, but in a different way, and unquestionably fabulous.

"I think I love this, too," I said, turning back to my mirror.

"It's really pretty," agreed my sister. "You won't really get to wear a dress like this ever again."

"Do you want to try it with the skirt that goes over top?" the saleswoman asked.

What! A secret skirt? Yes!

The tulle skirt went over the sequined skirt and fastened at the waist. Unlike most bridal wear, everything by Reem Acra is incredibly light. Instead of feeling weighed down by it, you feel like you're being lifted up like a heavenly angel. I tried the dress with and without the skirt, with and without the veil, probably fifteen times. I just didn't know which I liked better, this or the sexy asymmetrical ivory compression stocking.

Longchamp bag came over to investigate my progress.

"That's really pretty," she said. "Are you going to get that?"

"I don't know, I can't decide," I told her.

"Well, it's gorgeous," she said with a pained look in her eye that suggested she didn't understand that she could find things she also actually liked if she didn't try only to dress the way her mom wanted her to.

After much frolicking about in the sequined Cinderella number, I put the asymmetrical lace dress back on. And I just knew.

"I like this better. This is it," I said. I had spent my formative years almost exclusively in bodycon clothing, and now was not the time to turn back. I could wear a traditional dress or something tighter and fabulous, and I just had to choose the latter. I want a dress I will look back on when I'm forty-five and think, *I don't know how I wore something so slim-cut, white, and unforgiving, but I'm sure glad I got that out of my system.*

I put the veil on one more time. I was in love. This dress had put a ring on me. My mom held her palms up because there really were no words for it.

I never want to wear anything but this dress, I thought.

This, I finally understood, was the feeling fashion people have when they see a perfect pair of ripped tights. This was the fabulous product of impeccable, creative design. This was, for me, Fashion. It was exactly what a perfect dress should be: it made me feel like the best version of myself. You can look at Fashion as clothes by the absurd, for the even more absurd (and absurdity should be mocked or, at the very least, questioned). But you can also look at the ways these clothes—made by dedicated, passionate, and, yes, sometimes slightly crazy people—can make you feel like your best self, whether you're going to the mall, Fashion Week, or your own wedding.

Reem Acra will always hold a special place in my heart. And, because preserved wedding dresses take up so much room, a huge space in my closet.

That said, I'm definitely not losing my shit over an asymmetrical designer vest anytime soon.

10 Absolutely Vital Tips
for Everyone Who Wants to Work in Fashion

Unless you're the spawn of someone famous, fashion is never just going to invite you over for a cup of tea, so if you want to join, just barge right in and serve yourself with these pointers.

1. **When you first start out, always act like you know what's going on.** You *won't* know what's going on ever, but naïveté is not looked upon fondly in this industry. You will wonder, *Why are they all wearing sunglasses inside? Why are ninety photographers taking pictures of the girl wearing a dress over her pants?* But just pretend like you understand everything and this is all perfectly normal. And if you feel really confused, leave your sunglasses on so you can stare at everything weird around you.

2. **When you have been doing this for a while, always act like you don't know what's going on.** You used to be able to go to a fashion show without eighty million

people photographing each other at every corner. The runways used to be so creative, and now it's all one homogenous sea of easygoing Céline wannabe pants and neoprene sweatshirts. "I just don't understand it," you tell anyone who will listen. To really prove your point, leave your cell phone in your bag at Fashion Week, in defiance of all that social media has ruined.

3. **When in doubt, wear something simple.** You will often be confronted with talented dressers who can wear dresses over pants, and not in an "Eileen Fisher mom whose bed sheets are made from recycled materials" kind of way, but a "Givenchy runway model dressing from the future" kind of way. You will go home and try to re-create these masterful outfits only to realize you can't and look dumb like this. Instead, just wear a blazer over a jaunty tank with an understated necklace, a flattering jean, and a heel. You already look more chic than the people wearing two outfits at once.

4. **When really, *really* in doubt, wear all black.*** It's hard to wear an all-black outfit that makes you look completely unstylish. People will think you're one of those people who care more about the clothes around you than the clothes you're wearing, which is the hallmark of a true Fashion person.

5. **Don't post photos of yourself everywhere if it feels "off-brand."** Like it or not, if you have social media accounts, you have a "personal brand." A lot of people

---

* Unless you're going for a job interview with Anna Wintour, in which case you should put this book down and get your ass to a museum right now.

don't seem to know what to do with these accounts except act like celebrities, who are brainwashed by all of us into thinking they're the greatest, which is why they post selfies from their cars and airplane seats all day. But! You don't have to post selfies from your mundane daily activities! You don't even have to talk about yourself much! If you're not comfortable with making your feeds all about your face, then use them to share pictures of people or things or cats *around* you, or witty quotes or funny links. If you're not a Kardashian, you don't have to act like one.

6. **Work hard.** I know I know, this is cliché advice and I'm not your mom, so why don't I tell you something you don't know? Well, guess what? A lot of you don't know you have to work hard. *Really* hard. You can often tell you're working hard by whether or not you're sacrificing something. It might be sleep, it might be a dinner out with your friends, it might be a weekend away with your family. To succeed in a highly competitive field like fashion, you have to make sacrifices. The good thing about this is, if you are completely obsessed with what you do and want a fashion career so badly it hurts your soul, then you won't feel like you're sacrificing anything.

7. **Fear means you're doing your job.** Someone who works in fashion once said if you're scared all the time that means you're doing your job. And in a business built upon risk taking, you should take risks so big they scare you. And if your own risks don't scare you, the egos in this business are so delicate that it's not unlikely someone will get mad at you in a scary way at some point or another. So *embrace it*, or you just won't survive.

8. **Check your ego at the door.** Here's something they don't tell you before you get into this business: you can't spell fashion without "ego" (the "eg" is silent). Starting out typically involves working for one of these egos. And when you're working for an ego, there is no room for *your* ego. So check it at the door when you get to work, because if you want people to listen to you and respect your views, you have to earn it by keeping your head down and working hard until people see you as an angel who makes their lives easier. Until you earn respect, you have to treat your ego like the sweatsuit you put on when you get home after a long day: it's something only you have to know about. Make other people look good, make other people more successful, and you will become more successful.

9. **Beg for work.** Ears don't pierce themselves, and jobs won't fall into your lap. If you want something, you have to go out and ask for it. And in a competitive industry like fashion, you'll probably have to beg for it. You'll get rejected by your idol and have to go back to that person for more. But don't see it as demoralizing: a career you really, really, *really* want is totally worth a little groveling. And if you think it's not, then you probably don't want this as badly as you'll need to in order to get through it.

10. **Put your cell phone down and enjoy yourself.** This is a fun-ass business. You will spend a lot of time around the world's most beautiful clothes and the world's most beautiful and eccentric people at superfun parties with lots of free, delicious champagne and itsy-bitsy cupcakes. Enjoy yourself. Eat the cupcakes.

Acknowledgments

Thanks, first of all, go to my parents, whose kindness is immeasurable. I owe so much to my father, the funniest person I have ever known and will ever know. Thanks for passing down your sense of humor. I owe equally as much to my mom. Your amazing strength has always been an inspiration. Thank you, also, for passing down your proclivity for strong opinions, which I am told from time to time I've inherited. Thanks to both of my parents for being there for me every time I felt discouraged, and being more excited about this book than anyone, except for maybe my husband, Rick.

Rick, thank you for reading countless drafts and your ceaseless encouragement during my frequent bouts of self-doubt. Thank you also for coming around to my sweatpants, seeing as if you hadn't we might not be happily married, here, in the first place.

I am also incredibly grateful for the support of the rest of my family, especially my sister, Holly (who helped me pick out my wedding dress) and brother-in-law, Mark (who carefully steamed it the day before my wedding). Thanks also to the Goldbergs, Montis, and Friedmans for continually expressing excitement about this project over the several years it took to complete.

ACKNOWLEDGMENTS

Many people tried to force this book to be something it wasn't. Gillian Mackenzie and Karyn Marcus were not among them. Thank you both so much for believing in this project and sharing my vision for it. You were hard to find in my quest to publish this book, but the wait was well worth it.

Emily Graff edited this book with not only diligence and skill but also a lot of care and thoughtfulness. Thanks so much, Emily, for all your hard work and dedication to this project, bringing out the best in these essays, and making this book what it is. Working with you was a joy.

Finally, thanks to all my colleagues and various bosses who have believed in me over the years: Ben Williams and Adam Moss at *New York* mag; Troy Young, Joanna Coles, Kate Lewis, and David Carey at Hearst; and my entire team at Cosmopolitan.com.

And finally, I am incredibly grateful to all my friends who have been there for me over the years. Without so many of you, I'd not only be kind of miserable, but also, much more poorly dressed.

About the Author

Amy Odell is the editor of Cosmopolitan.com, the largest community of millennial women on the Internet. In 2015, Odell was named to *Forbes'* list of "30 Under 30" in media and featured in *Adweek* as a "New Publisher," one of fifteen young innovators who will change the magazine business. In 2014, she appeared in Crain's "40 Under 40." Prior to Cosmopolitan.com, Odell was an editor at BuzzFeed from 2012 through 2013. Odell began her journalism career in 2007 as a party reporter for *New York* magazine, where she ultimately became the founding blogger of the magazine's fashion blog, The Cut, in 2008. A native of Austin, Odell graduated from New York University and lives in Tribeca with her husband and very sassy cat.